The Truths, Insights, Laws, Revelations of Human Beings and of God

Understanding Kingdom Principles in Life

KRISTEN MARIE PLAYER

Ordering Information:

Prime Seven Media
518 Landmann St.
Tomah City, WI 54660

Printed in the United States of America

Table of Contents

Religious Quotes Book 1

 hen you believe and have faith in God. That's when things will start to happen. God is the solution to all of your problems. What you suffer with the most will bring you closer and stronger to God. God allows you to suffer for you to know him. God will reveal to you all of God's insights and revelations through your greatest pain and suffering. The life of the holy spirit from God that is within you will take away all of your sicknesses despairs sorrows addictions hurts.

Your biggest lessons come from your greatest sorrows. You learn your most important and valuable and greatest lessons. Through experiencing your greatest pain and suffering. Your most difficult battles teach you the truths insights laws revelations of God. You are fulfilling the journey of your life that God has created for you. God has lots of amazing blessings to reward you with. Everything you are wanting to see happen in your life. God will make happen in God's Perfect and Amazing Timing. God knows what you struggle with and suffer with the most in your life. Shall you know that God will save you and rescue you from everything.

God will give you all of God's power control strength courage. To help you to conquer your most impossible problems sickness addictions grief. When you feel stuck in a rut with your problems. Know that God is on your side the whole way. God will comfort you in times of despair and sadness. God will uplift your spirits in times of sorrow and hurt. God will always bless you and love you forevermore. When people do you wrong by being unfair towards you. Know that you have got a Faithful Just Loving Caring Compassionate Father God who absolutely loves you and adores you. The void that is missing within you is where God dwells within you. Through the power of the holy spirit. God will give you the strength and the will to do everything that you want to do.

Jesus Christ Almighty died on the cross to save you from your sins. By giving you the gift of Eternal Life in The Paradise of Heaven with God. God knows your deepest wounds and hurts. Shall you know that God will restore save deliver heal cure your soul from everything. God will deliver rescue break all of your chains set you totally free. From all of your problems addictions sickness heartache pain grief. God knows the pain and suffering you are in. Trust in and have faith in God. That God will heal you and save you. God has got all of the control and power over everyone in this world. God will be with you until the end of the world.

God will exalt uplift bless reward fulfill prosper your spirit. God will bless you with God's love joy peace happiness truths laws. God will solve all of your problems for you. God has got a solution to every problem you have. With God everything is possible but without God everything is impossible. God loves you beyond your comprehension. God loves you beyond your understanding. God loves you more than you can fathom. Everything you go through in your life. God has got a miraculous plan and purpose for you. God will forever and always take you to the places. You have always wished to be in. With God there will always be hope.

The more positive joyful peaceful happy we become in ourselves. The easier it will be to conquer our bad habits. God knows what saddens you and causes you grief and heartache. God will bless you and reward you. By making your life a whole lot better. In every great way. God knows everything about you. God knows all of your troubles sorrows despairs hurts sadness. You go through God will always comfort you and reassure your spirits. When you have a relationship with God. God will bless reward fulfill prosper sustain purify your soul totally. God's truths insights laws revelations will set you totally free. God will bless you with independence freedom positivity.

There is power liberation freedom in having a relationship with God. God can do the impossible what you can't do in your life. When you reach out to God. Then God will reach out to you. God has got big blessings for you to receive. The closer and stronger your faith in God becomes. The more your unwanted bad habits will push themselves out of your life. When you walk in The Lord Jesus Christ Almighties ways. You will see how The Lord Jesus Christ will transform your life for the better.

God is a lot more powerful than your problems addictions sickness pain suffering. God will wipe away all of your impossible challenges. God will get you through all of your battles and difficultes because God absolutely cares about you and cherishes you completely. God will bless you with all of. The positivity and enthusiasm to live a joyful peaceful content happy truthful and a rewarding life. No problem is impossible for God to conquer. God can and God will conquer all of your battles for you. Always be with people who accept you and appreciate you.

Who don't judge you. Who love you and who you can trust. When you talk about your faith in God with other people. God will bless you and reward you doubly. God will bring to you the right people in your life. Who will treasure cherish appreciate love adore you. What we struggle with and suffer with the most. Helps us to gain God's special knowledge. All of your problems addictions sickness hardships hurts upsets. Are there to teach you all of the lessons. That God wants to reveal to you. God will open up your spirit into all of God's. Unconditional love grace integrity mercy respect goodness enlightenment. We need to be respectful kind loving good to people. Who are unkind uncaring unfair towards us. You are more priviledged and advantaged. When you are close to God and when you know God very well.

Always find your identity in The Lord Jesus Christ Almighty. Through the power of the holy spirit. Don't find your identity in people. God is an unconditionally loving kind good forgiving compassionate sympathetic righteous accepting fair just Eternal God. When people hurt you and disappoint you and let you down. Know with all of your heart and soul that your Father God in Heaven loves you. Don't allow yourself to be in despair and frustrated. God has got a beautiful and a rewarding purpose for you in your life.

God has got your whole life in God's hands. You are in God's capable hands always and forevermore. God will never ever let you go. Always put all of your trust hope faith belief love in God. God's love for you will last for all of Eternity. On Earth and in The Paradise of Heaven forever to come forevermore. When you feel trapped in your problems. Know that God will remove your problems. In God's Perfect Timing. God will heal bless reward guide restore replenish you. Build you up and make you strong and courageous. God knows everything that burdens you and causes you heartache and grief.

God will always be there to give you comfort hope courage. God is teaching you your most greatest valuable important lessons. Through experiencing your biggest pain and suffering. Through all of your trials and tribulations God will forever and always. Bless you and reward you with God's joy peace happiness. God will make all of your dreams come true always and forevermore. God will answer all of your prayers in God's Amazing Timing. God knows and God understands how much you struggle and suffer with your most difficult battles. God will help you to be victorious. God has overcome the world by sending Jesus to die on the cross. To save you from your sins. No problem is impossible for God to conquer. You are fulfilling the purpose of your life that God has chosen for you.

God has lots of surprises delights rewards blessings for you. God will take away all of your inhibitions that are holding you back. God will make you strong uplifted empowered. God will heal cure save restore deliver you from your sicknesses brokenheartedness despairs sorrows hurts sadness. When people hurt you with hurtful words. Forgive them and understand that they are feeling wounded within themselves. God knows all of your worries hurts upsets grief. That other people cause you.

God will make your life a lot better. God will fulfill all of your needs wants desires wishes longings yearnings of your heart. God will bless you and love you forever and ever. Your faith and trust in God will help you to overcome surpass conquer achieve accomplish. Your impossible problems addicitons sickness heartache pain despairs. Hand over all of your pain and suffering to. The Lord Jesus Christ Almighty. Jesus Christ will sooth ease comfort support love care for you. When you have a relationship with God. God will reveal to you God's amazing incredible insightful truths laws revelations.

In Jesus Christ we are overcomers and conquerers through all of our problems. Jesus will carry you through everything. Move on from people who mistreat you badly. There are lots of great and amazing people for you to be friends with in this world. When people hurt blame mistreat you badly. Seize opportunities to make better friends. When you accept The Lord Jesus Christ Almighty as your Lord and Saviour. Jesus Christ will give you the power of the holy spirit within your heart and soul. God won't let you stay down for too long. God will uplift elate exalt your spirits. To the highest heights of disappoint you let you down. Know that God will make your life a whole lot better. God has got plans to bless prosper reward fulfill sustain help heal deliver save set you totally free from everything.

One day you will be in The Paradise of Heaven with God. God will make you perfect in God's Image. You will be with God forever and ever. When there is life there will always be hope for all of us. God is going to bless you and reward you with an exciting future. God will lead you to the right places for you to meet the right people. Who will become your lifelong friends. God is strengthening your faith and trust in God. Through experiencing your biggest battles.

The way you treat yourself and other people determines your own fate and destiny. God has got big plans to prosper bless reward fulfill sustain you. God is always with you through everything. It is so much better to always treat people with respect kindness goodness forgiveness compassion fairness than to hurt people. God will open up new doors in your life. For exciting possibilities and opportunities to happen for you. Always have friends who treat you with respect kindness goodness fairness justness compassion empathy. Choose your friends very carefully and wisely. Not everyone will be good for you. God knows all of the desires of your heart. God will grant you all of the desires of your heart in God's Perfect Timing.

God will give you all of the power strength courage. To help you to conquer your most impossible problems addictions sickness heartache grief. Always have friends who are genuine sincere honest trustworthy. Positive kind good loving fair people. Will attract these types of people to them in their lives. God knows and God understands everything you struggle with and suffer with. God will give you the power to conquer your battles. God will turn your whole life around for the better. God has got amazing incredible delights surprises rewards to bless you with. God has big plans to prosper restore bless reward you with abundantly. Always have positive contented peaceful joyful happy kind good fair love in all of your relationships.

God will heal cure restore replenish deliver save set you totally free from your sicknesses diseases sins trials tribulations. A husband and wife who both have a close relationship with God. Are very blessed advantaged lucky privileged in their marriage. God will comfort you in times of despair and sadness. God will uplift your spirits in times of sorrow and hurt. God will always bless you and love you unconditionally. God is going to bless reward inspire exalt uplift enlighten empower your spirits big time for all of Eternity.

God will bring new people into your life. Who have a close relationship with God. Who will become your closest and truest friends. God will uplift elate exalt bless reward your spirit. God knows everything you go through. God is your rock and refuge. God loves you beyond your comprehension. God loves you beyond your understanding. God loves you more than you can fathom. No matter how hard you are struggling and suffering with trying to conquer your problems. Know that God will make you victorious one day. In God's Perfect and Majestic Timing. In good time God will heal all of your wounds.

God is your Provider Restorer Deliverer Refuge Saviour. God is your only hope. God will make you totally lucky fortunate blessed privileged. God loves you abundantly. God is always on your side through everything you will ever go through. God will give you all of the positivity hope focus motivation strength courage for you to live a well grounded healthy peaceful joyful happy go lucky life. God's love is infinitely more powerful than any of our problems. God's love will always win. God's love will conquer everything always and forever. God will heal restore save rescue deliver unleash all of your chains totally. From all of your sicknesses hurts burdens sadness sorrows. God thinks about you all of the time. God is always with you wherever you go.

God knows your needs before you do. God will bless you and love you. God's love conquers everything. God's love will always win. God's love is the answer to everything. God is going to bless you and reward you abundantly. With great and amazing friends who will be your best and closest friends forever. God is going to perform an instant miracle on you. By removing out of your life your unhealthy habits. God's unconditional love joy peace happiness kindness goodness fairness. Overrides our difficult challenges.

God is going to bless you abundantly each new day you live your life. God wants to provide for you all of your needs. God will bless you and reward you abundantly. With excellent health emotionally physically spiritually mentally always and forevermore. God has got all of the right best good reasons purposes. Why you struggle and suffer with your problems. God will never ever let you go. You are in the capable hands of God. God has got lots of plans to bless reward prosper you. Eventually your long lived addictions will fall away and disappear into nothing. Your addictions will drop away naturally on there own.

In The Paradise of Heaven God will give you a new healthy spiritual heavenly body. God will make you Perfect in God's Image. God is going to perform big miracles on your emotional and physical health always and forevermore. With faith and trust in God. By having your own perserverance persistance patience. Everything can be achieved surpassed conquered. With God everything is possible but without God everything is impossible. God has got your future all worked out perfectly. God allows us to suffer and struggle with our problems. For us to grow stronger deeper closer richer more powerfully in our faith in God. God is going to heal and cure you from everything that is holding you back. God's love is infinitely more greater than your problems.

God always blesses and rewards God's children who are positive kind loving good fair just. What you struggle with and suffer with the most. God will strengthen you and bless you. With God's insights laws revelations. By bringing you closer to God. Your victorious and triumphant day will come very soon. Where God will set you totally free from all of your problems addictions sickness sadness despairs grief. Nothing is impossible to God. God will make you victorious over your most impossible problems. What you battle with the most teaches you and guides you to God's special knowledge.

Take that giant leap of faith by stepping out of your comfort zone. To conquer your battles. You learn and grow the most. With your faith love hope in God. With what you struggle with and suffer with the most in your life. All of your battles teach you all about God's laws. That God wants to reveal to you always and forevermore. God will remove all difficulties problems addictions despairs hurts sadness. In your life God will bless you big time. God knows so well how much you are struggling and suffering. With trying to conquer your battles. God will always help you love you and bless you. God knows everything about you. God understands all of your battles. God will make you victorious and triumphant through everything.

Your battles that you are finding most difficult to conquer. God will give you all of the power strength courage for you to be victorious through it all. God will make your life exciting great worthwhile rewarding awe-inspiring meaningful enlightening. Always associate yourself with people who are positive loving kind good fair just.

You become like the people who you associate with the most. Going through your greatest pain and suffering. You learn grow develop. Your biggest important valuable greatest lessons. Your most impossible battles that you are really struggling with and suffering with to overcome. God will rescue and save you from.

God knows and God understands how hard your life can be at certain times. God will prosper you and bless you in your life. One day your bright magical miraculous supernatural happy day will come. Where God will set you totally free from your problems. God's respect compassion love goodness kindness forgiveness. Reigns all over the Earth and in The Kingdom of Heaven for all of Eternity. God can move the biggest mountains in your life. God can do the impossible for you. God can do what you can't do. God is delivering you gradually bit by bit. Every day step by step. From your most impossible battles.

With faith and trust in God and the right attitude. With a positive outlook. God will conquer all of your problems. God will strengthen you by making you so. Strong empowering enlightening awe-inspiring truthful. In God's Perfect Image. You learn grow mature the most from experiencing your greatest pain suffering sorrows struggles. God will bring to you the right best amazing people. Who will have a close relationship with God. Who will become your great lifelong friends. God will use God's miraculous supernatural wholesome magical magnificent powers. To fix you totally from everything in your life. God is going to lead you to amazing meaningful opportunities possibilities.

For you to live a secure and a happy future. God will bless you and reward you. With God's joy peace excitement love hope happiness. Through all of your trials and tribulations. Having pain and suffering is a normal part of being a human being. We grow and learn with our faith in God through our pain and suffering. In the right and best time. God will remove all of your impossible struggles and battles. Always hold onto strongly by keeping your faith love hope in God. God works through you the most when you are experiencing your greatest pain and suffering. Come to God with your burdens sorrows addictions depairs pain suffering struggles strongholds. God will deliver you and set you totally free from everything.

You become closer deeper stronger more powerful in your faith love hope in God. Through experiencing your worst experiences. Open up your heart and soul to God. God will reveal to you everything you need to know in your life. You gain all of God's special knowledge through experiencing your greatest pain and suffering. God is making you Almighty and Courageous through experiencing your bad times. God will do great and amazing things to those people. Who believe in God. God is all powerful all knowing. God can do anything.

Always treat people in positive kind hearted good willed fair just ways. Then God will bless you and reward you abundantly always and forevermore. God has got all of the power. To perform supernatural miraculous magical miracles on you in every area of your life. God made you out of star dust in your mother's womb. God knows everything about you. God will help you in every way in your life. God allows us to suffer with and struggle with our long lived problems sickness addictions heartache pain grief. To bring us into God's Kingdom of God's knowledge. In God's Perfect and Outstanding Timing. God will take your spirit into The Paradise of Heaven.

Where you will dwell in Heaven with God and your past dearly loved ones for all of Eternity. God will heal cure restore replenish deliver rescue save set you totally free from all of your painful problems. With God there is always positivity and hope. For a better more rewarding tomorrow. God will bless you with God's magnificent enlightenment. God is forever and always healing us from all of our problems sicknesses diseases sorrows despairs hurts upsets grievances. From our past. Be your own person and don't follow the crowd. Find your own identity in The Lord Jesus Christ Almighty. God is amazingly incredibly awesome great brilliant supernaturally majestic divine righteous pure innocent magnificent.

God will intervene within you by removing all of your impossible battles and struggles. God will always bless you and love you forevermore. God allows us to have problems and to suffer. To draw our strength in more powerful ways. To bring us closer to God. God will heal and cure you totally from all of your sicknesses addictions anguishes sorrows sadness despairs. Always focus on God don't let yourself be consumed by your own problems. You will be a lot more joyful positive happier. God will make us Perfect in God's Image. When we are in The Paradise of Heaven. Everyone everywhere everything will be Perfect and Completely Blissful forevermore.

There will be no more pain suffering sorrows struggles hardships difficulties addictions sadness grief. When we are in The Kingdom of Heaven. The most important reason why we have been given the gift of life. Is to have a relationship with God. God will make possible for you to conquer your most difficult battles. With God everything is possible to overcome. God uses your weaknesses bad problems hurts upsets sadness. For God to turn all of your bad problems around into your own favour for your own good.

God will forever and always turn your worst experiences. Into your best experiences. God will always turn your bad times into your good times. God is going to pour out God's miraculous cleansing healing purifying powers. To save you totally from everything that troubles you and burdens you. Always work hard at improving and bettering yourself. Through all of your obstacles weaknesses difficulties you go through. There are good and right reasons and purposes why you struggle and suffer with what you do. God will make you stronger wiser better. God is an unconditionally loving kind good fair just accepting understanding compassionate forgiving meaningful truthful non-judgemental God.

You learn grow mature become stronger closer more powerful in God. Through experiencing your greatest pain and suffering. Always associate with the right people. Don't associate with the wrong people. Always love accept be kind be good be wise be comfortable within yourself. Be your own best friend. God is going to bless you and reward you abundantly. With a prosperous truthful exciting meaningful adventurous wonderful future. God will comfort you in times of distress and sadness. You are very lucky fortunate blessed privileged. When you have a relationship with God.

Always maintain a calm settled stable positive focused well grounded forgiving accepting and a happy outlook. With God everything is possible but without God everything is impossible. Hallelujah Praise The Lord Jesus Christ Almighty. Don't put your expectations and hopes in people. Always put your expectations and hopes in your Faithful Loving Righteous Father God Almighty. God will renew uplift exalt build up transform bless reward your spirit. God's love for you will last for all of Eternity. On Earth and in Heaven. You are growing developing learning becoming more knowledgeable. Through experiencing your most difficult battles.

The only thing in the end that matters the most in life. Is to have trust belief hope faith love in your Supreme Majestic Righteous Magnifcent Father God Almighty. God is the most important reason why we all exist on this Earth. God knows you better than you know yourself. God knows you better than anyone else knows you. God will always find a way for you out of your bad problems. Keep your faith love hope in God. Never stop believing in God. The more you focus on God. The more you will gain God's qualities attributes charactaristics. You can never go wrong with God. God will lead you to like minded people. Who will become your faithful trusted reliable closest best friends.

Never react to the cruelty of other people. Always show your respect compassion sympathy empathy kindness goodness love fairness forgiveness to people like this. God will keep your wellbeing healthy sane together well balanced strong positive joyful peaceful happy. God will always perform the biggest miraculous supernatural amazing miracles and wonders on you. For you to surpass all of your trials. God has got your life all planned out perfectly. God blesses you and rewards you according to the intentions of your heart.

God has got lots of exciting great amazing places for you to go to. God has got a lot of wonderful people that you will meet. Your love in God will carry you through everything you will ever endure on this Earth. From the beginning and until the end of your time on this Earth. Everyone is overcome by some impossible problem addiction sickness disease heartache grief. God will make it possible for you to be courageous by conquering your painful problems. That you are stuck in. When people are cruel to you. Know that you have got an Unconditionally Loving Gracious Majestic Glorious Father God. Who absolutely loves you and adores you.

God will bless you and reward you with God's excellent enlightenment empowerment insights truths laws revelations always and forevermore. God will always fulfill sustain bless reward guide restore replenish help save you from your sins. You will win friends positively. When you are respectful kind hearted good willed loving compassionate sympathetic empathetic to people. Your faith love hope in God. Will keep you well emotionally physically spiritually mentally. God will always bless you and love you. God is forever and always with you through sickness and health. God will heal transform restore make you strong save your health. God will turn your whole life around for the better because God absolutely loves you and adores you.

God's love for you is infinitely more powerful. Than any problem addiction sickness heartache despair sorrow pain suffering. God is moving out from you your deepest wounds. God is blessing you abundantely with God's peace joy happiness through your pain. God will bless you and reward you immensely when you always follow. God's commandents of the holy spirit from God. At every moment of every day. God is perfecting you changing you transforming you. For the better in God's Perfect Image. God is shaping you moulding you helping you building you up making you powerful. Through your hardest problems addictions sickness heartache pain grief.

No matter what problem you have been experiencing. Know and trust with all of your heart. That God will make a way out of your trials. God will make you fearless lucky unafraid fortunate blessed honoured privileged for all of Eternity. When you go through your own adversity. Know that God will make you victorious and triumphant. God will love you when you are hurting. God will comfort you in times of sorrow. God will exalt your spirits when you are down. God will work through you and other people. To heal save help support guide bless reward prosper Glorify your soul forever and ever.

God will give you independence freedom positivity. When you always do kind loving good deeds for everyone. Always be respectful considerate positive kind good loving fair just forgiving to everyone. If you stay faithful devoted committed to God. Then God will stay faithful devoted committed to you. Always be loving to unloving people. Be fair to unfair people. Be kind to unkind people. Be just to unjust people. Always look for the positivity goodness beauty in other people. Don't have friends who treat you unfairly. God will comfort you in times of despair. God will bless you with God's mercy grace respect compassion love. Through your darkest moments.

God will bless you and reward you abundantely with the highest degree of ecstacy of joy excitement peace positivity happiness. When you conquer your battles. God will forever and always help you to be victorious triumphant powerful strong willed courageous through everything. God will make possible for you to conquer your impossible problems addictions battles sickness struggles suffering grief. Always rise above the cruelty negativity judgements of other people. God will save your soul through everything always and forevermore. Never judge anyone with what they suffer with.

Always be accepting understanding compassionate sympathetic non-judgemental. When you always do the right thing. By being positive kind loving good fair to everyone. Then God will bless you big time.

God will always bless you and reward you abundantely. With God's supernatural love kindness goodness integrity everlasting peace joy happiness forevermore. God will bless you and reward you with joy peace excitement happiness hope love positivity. Through your trials troubles burdens tribulations. When people mistreat you unfairly. Know that God will comfort you reassure you and make you feel better.

God really appreciates adores cherishes treasures nutures cares about you and loves you very much. God will fulfill all of your hearts desires. That you have so long to see come to fruition. In God's Perfect and Majestic Timing. With God there will always be hope for a better positive peaceful joyful happy rewarding meaningful future. God will give you the strength power courage for you to cope really well with all of your problems. God will set you totally free from everything always and forever. God will give you the positivity freedom hope strength to succeed with all of your ambitions goals dreams in your life.

The stronger and positive our faith love hope is God becomes. The easier our difficult problems will be to conquer. God will always heal save rescue deliver unleash all of your chains set you totally free from all of your past hurts traumas upsets. God will give you everything you are looking for in your life. God loves you beyond your comprehension. When you forgive and love people who mistreat you unfairly. Then God will forgive and love you. You grow and learn the most. Through experiencing your most challenging problems.

God will wipe away all of your addictions sickness brokeness illness struggles pain suffering always and forevermore.

Don't ever hurt anyone unfairly. Always treat people well with respect consideration kindness love goodness compassion fairness empathy sympathy. God will make fresh starts and new beginnings. When you get through your trials troubles burdens tribulations hurts. Through your darkest moments God will shine God's brightest becon of light. To save rescue heal deliver you from your deepest despairs. The way you treat other people is how you are going to be treated in return. All of us will always reap what we will sow forevermore. Always build people up in positive and empowering ways.

Never tear anyone down in negative and disempowering ways. God loves you and cares about you that much. That God wants to step in into your life. By healing you from everything. God will make you happy when you are sad. God will help you when you feel hopeless. God will love you when you are hurting. God will bless you with respect positivity dignity grace. When you always do the right thing by other people. Always bring out the best in people. By uplifting their spirits. Never bring anyone down. God will comfort you in times of despair. God will exalt your spirits when you are down. God will always be there for you through everything. God will always guide you to the richness of God's Wisdom Honour Glory forevermore.

God knitted you in your mother's womb. All of us are God's Creation. God is always perfecting your ways throughout Eternity. The more powerful your faith love hope in God becomes. God will make it more manageable and bearable for you to conquer your battles. In the bible God said that God has promised a way out of all of your problems and temptations. There is a light at the end of every tunnel. Every grey cloud has got a silver lining. When there is a will there will always be a way. God will heal transform sanctify cleanse your soul. Through all of your trials troubles burdens hurts upsets tribulations.

God will wipe away all of your impossible battles addictions sickness suffering pain illness grief. God will heal you from everything. In The Paradise of Heaven everyone everywhere everything will be Perfect Glorious Righteous Graceful Pure Majestic in God's Image. God loves you and adores you more than you can ever imagine. God will save your soul through everthing you will ever experience. When people hurt you unfairly love them. When people reject you forgive them. When people don't accept you pray for them. God has got all of the power to heal us from everything we experience in our lives.

If you keep on persevering persisting being patient by never ever giving up. God will deliver you from everything. God has got all of the power to conquer all of your difficult problems. From the beginning and until the end of your time on this Earth. God has got plans to prosper bless fulfill inspire help support guide love encourage you always and forevermore. Your most challenging problems teach you your greatest valuable important lessons. With God on your side you will be able to get through all of your trials troubles burdens tribulations forever and ever. You grow learn advance develop become stronger wiser better positive closer to God. When you go through your most difficult battles.

One day God will make possible what you are finding impossible to conquer. Never ever give up. You will make it through everything. God knows so well everything that you struggle with in your life. God will make you victorious triumphant powerful through it all. If you never ever lose hope by never ever giving up. Then eventually you will win outgrow conquer all of your battles. God will bless you through sickness and health. You are always in God's capable hands. God always protects God's believers. Having a relationship with God is the whole purpose of our existance.

Always stay close to God and God will always stay close to you. The more powerful your faith love hope in God becomes. The stronger happier better settled saner calmer resilient you will cope. God will help you to win all of your battles. God loves you more than you can ever imagine. God will make everything better for you. In God's Perfect and Amazing Timing. God will answer all of your prayers. God will always bless love save your soul. God will help you to stay on top of everything you will ever experience. God will bless you and reward you through sickness and health.

God knows your needs before you do. God knows you better than you know yourself. God knows you better than anyone else knows you. With God on your side you can do everything and anything. God will give you the power strength courage for you to achieve all of your dreams. Always walk closely with God and then God will always walk closely with you. God made you the way you are. Never compare yourself to anyone else. God has given you your own strengths gifts qualities talents. God will comfort you in times of despair. God will love you when you are hurting. God will exalt your soul always and forevermore. God will turn your weaknesses into your strengths.

God will always be able to conquer all of your challenging problems. God will heal all of your wounds of your past present future. God will bless reward fulfill uplift prosper exalt build you up always in your spirits. God will make a way out of your impossible problems addictions battles sickness. When you feel like there is no way out. God will give you all of the positivity strength hope you need to succeed by being triumphant through all of your battles. God is your Rock Healer Deliverer Helper Saviour Answer to all of your Prayers Redeemer Source of Strength Life Line.

When you always do kind loving good deeds for everyone. God will bless you and reward you. With good luck good fortune success. God blesses you and rewards you. According to the intentions of your heart. Always show your compassion love forgiveness to everyone. God will do what you can't do. God will make possible with what you are finding impossible to conquer. God will save your soul forever and ever. We are always conquerers and overcomers in The Lord Jesus Christ Almighty. God will make you victorious courageous triumphant through everything. God sees everything you do and say. God is always with you perfecting your ways through everything you do and say.

Always learn from all of the mistakes you make. Always treat people well with respect consideration compassion sympathy empathy forgiveness love kindness goodness fairness justness. Try your very best not to hurt anyone. God will bless you abundantely then. As you grow older. You get use to the battles that God puts you through. When you develop better knowledge experience resources to cope in your life. God will renew help support encourage make you strong inspired empowered insightful through everything. God will set your soul completely free from everything always and forevermore. With God you will always succeed with everything you want to.

Always be with people who are respectful considerate positive kind hearted good willed compassionate sympathetic empathetic forgiving loving faithful devoted committed. Who have a close relationship with God. Always be quick to love and forgive people who hurt you unfairly. Never hold any grudges towards anyone. God will forever and always bless reward comfort love forgive empower reassure prosper restore exalt Glorify your soul forevermore. God loves you more than you can fathom. God will heal you from all of your troubles despairs sorrows burdens.

When people aren't always there for you. God is always with you so closely. God is always giving you all of the desires of your heart forevermore. God will heal fix save rescue prosper all of your relationships with everyone in your family and friends. God will give you everything you are looking for in your life. God loves you beyond your comprehension. When people reject you forgive them. When people don't appreciate you love them. When people don't value you pray for them. God will take your spirit to The Paradise of Heaven. In God's Perfect and Outstanding Timing. Always hold onto your faith love hope in God.

God will bless and reward your health emotionally physically spiritually mentally always and forevermore. In The Paradise of Heaven with God. There will be no more suffering no more pain no more sickness no more sorrow no more grief. God will make your spirit Perfect in God's Image in The Paradise of Heaven for all of Eternity. Always bounce back quickly from the put downs that other people can put you through. When there is life there will always be hope for all of us. God will save deliver set you totally free from everything. God will make you life exciting worthwhile satisfying meaningful delightful rewarding truthful awe-inspiring thrilling. With God everything will always be possible. God will go on loving you forever. On Earth and in The Kingdom of Heaven for all Eternity.

When people are against you. Know in your heart and soul that God is always on your side. God loves you more than you can ever imagine. When life gets you down. Turn to your Faithful Majestic Loving Compassionate Father God Almighty. God will give you your life meaning purpose commitments truth trust genuine relationships. God will improve fulfill sustain transform refine replenish help support guide inspire encourage you. By making your life a whole lot better in every great way. Always seek God and God will bless you and reward you big time. God made you the way you are.

When people hurt you unfairly. Always pray a kind loving good prayer for people like this. God will bless love reward prosper empower restore uplift fulfill exalt build you up save Glorify your soul forevermore. Always open up your heart and soul to God. And then God will open up God's heart and soul to you. The way you treat yourself and other people. Determines your own fate and destiny. God will make possible what you are finding impossible to conquer. God will give you the power to be victorious through everything. With your faith hope love in God you will always win all of your most difficult battles. Your difficult battles are your way to God.

God will give you the courage to conquer all of your battles. In God's Perfect and Majestic Timing. God will bless you and reward you with joy peace happiness excitement hope love positivity. Through all of your trials burdens troubles tribulations. When people don't accept you pray for them. When people reject you forgive them. When people hurt you unfairly love them. Try try try again and you will succeed. If you never ever give up then you will always win and overcome all of your battles. Continue opening up your heart and soul to God. And God will cleanse purify rectify heal help restore all of your painful battles. God will heal you from all of your troubles and burdens. God is walking with you through your hardest problems. You are never alone.

Keep on perservering persisting being patient through all of your painful battles. God will set you totally free from all of your most difficult problems. In God's Perfect and Amazing Timing. The closer more real your faith hope love in God becomes. The stronger and healthier you will feel emotionally physically spiritually mentally. And the less complications you will have in your relationships. God has got all of the power and control over every person on this Earth. God will put you in a favourable situation in your life. When you are always with the right people who treat you well with respect kindness goodness love fairness. Then God will always bless you and reward you big time.

Your challenging problems are there to teach you bring you closer stronger deeper more powerful in God's love grace mercy compassion dignity respect. God has got for you. One day God will make a way out of your impossible battles sickness addictions heartache pain grief. When you are ready in God's Perfect and Majestic Timing. Always be respectful considerate loving kind good positive just fair to everyone. Always be with people who build you up who never tear you down. When you struggle with and suffer with problems that are beyond your ability to conquer.

Trust that God will find a way for you to be victorious triumphant courageous powerful through it all. Not everyone is going to like you and that's okay. Stick with those people who love accept value cherish adore treasure you completely. In this life you will only have a few complete compassionate just loving forgiving accepting connection with people. The negative opinions of other people shouldn't affect you in the slightest. It is more important what you believe about yourself to be true. Always rise above the negativity and cruelty of other people. Always forgive and love people who do you wrong. God will always love you and bless you forevermore. With God you can achieve surpass overcome conquer accomplish everything.

God will forever and always make you lucky fortunate blessed priveleged. On this Earth and in The Paradise of Heaven for all of Eternity. Always stand strong firm steady in your faith love hope in God. Don't ever let anyone take away your peace joy happiness. No matter what people try to do to you. Always keep your strong close deep powerful faith and trust in God. You will never go wrong. God will always protect you by keeping you safe wherever you go. Always think positive peaceful joyful happy lovely beautiful thoughts. Always forgive and love everyone. Who hurts you unfairly. Never hurt anyone. Always be positive kind loving good fair just to everyone.

Don't take any notice of the negativity and cruelty of other people. God will make you resilient loving forgiving centered. Never judge anyone with what they suffer with. Always show your compassion sympathy empathy warmth love kindness goodness fairness to everyone. God knows all of your sickness suffering brokeness battles bad health you are going through. God will save you victoriously. Sometimes people won't understand what you are going through. Know that God understands completely everything you experience. God knows all of your painful problems that you are going through.

Respect forgive love be kind be good to people who hurt you badly. Don't ever let anyone get to you. Always be strong courageous resilient brave enough to cope with people's cruelty. God will bless you and reward you abundantly. When you associate with the right and best people in your life. Sometimes God allows us to struggle with and suffer with our difficult problems. To prove our faith love trust hope in God. With God there will always be positivity hope joy peace happiness unconditional love kindness goodness integrity grace mercy for a bright and a rewarding future. God will bring into your life like minded people. Who will become your trusted and faithful lifelong friends.

People project onto you what is going on on the inside of themselves. It is not your problem when people mistreat you unfairly. It is their problem. All of us will reap what we will sow. Karma comes back to all of us. We grow learn become more insightful knowledgeable wiser well grounded closer to God. In our still and quite moments throughout our days. Always have friends who are genuine sincere honest trustworthy. Who you know you can completely rely upon. Who won't let you down. Who you can trust.

Sometimes God allows us to struggle with and suffer with painful problems. For us to open our hearts to God's special knowledge. God will bless you and reward you abundantly. When you associate with the right and best people in your life. When you respect people by doing positive kind loving good deeds. God will bless you and reward you big time. When people hurt you deeply. Understand that they are dealing with their own troubles burdens hurts upsets sadness despairs sorrows. All of us are going through our own difficult problems. God will comfort you in times of despair. God will bless you in times of sorrow.

God will uplift your spirits in times of sadness. God will answer your prayers in God's Perfect and Outstanding Timing. God will bring you God's peace joy hope happiness love to your soul. With faith and trust in God. Everything can be achieved overcome conquered surpassed accomplished. God will bring into your life the right people. Who will guide you to God's truths insights laws revelations and God's special knowledge. Stick with God and you will always get victory with everything you are going through. You are in the capable hands of God. God will transform and change you in God's Perfect Image. God will save your soul from everything. God always thinks about you 24/7 of every moment of every day and night you live.

The most important reason why we have been given the gift of life is to have a relationship with God. You earn your freedom independence privileges with the kind loving good deeds you do for people. God will make your impossible battles possible for you to conquer. In God's Supreme and Magnificent Timing. With God you will be victorious triumphant powerful through everything. God's truths and laws will always set you totally free. We are always learning our most important lessons through our most painful problems. God will pick you up every time you fall down.

God is your Rock Fortress Redeemer Deliverer Healer Helper Saviour through all of your trials and tribulations. God will remove all of your embedded and ingrained bad habits. That you are finding impossible to conquer. God can do anything and everything for you in your life. God is forever with you through all of your trials troubles burdens tribulations pain suffering. God will never ever let you go. In God's Perfect and Magnificent Timing. God will remove everything you have been longing to conquer and overcome in your life. God will perform instantaneous miraculous supernatural miracles and wonders on you.

To heal save rescue deliver restore you from everything. God can do everything for us that we can't do for ourselves. God has got all of the power strength courage to heal you from everything you are suffering with in your life. Hand over all of your worries to your Lord Jesus Christ Almighty. Your Lord Jesus will comfort you in times of distress. God will take good care of you. God will love you forever and ever. On Earth and in The Kingdom of Heaven for all of Eternity. God has got all of the complete control and power over everyone on this Earth. You are always in the capable hands of God. At every moment of every day of your life. God will never ever let you down. God will always make you fruitful blessed lucky fortunate privileged joyful peaceful happy go lucky forevermore.

With faith and trust in God everything is possible but without God everything is impossible. God especially blesses and rewards those people who have their hearts and souls open to God's word. Through the power of the holy spirit. Without God we are nothing. When you are down with your problems. Trust that God will turn you life around for the better. God will always bless love prosper your soul with joy peace happiness excitement exuberance forevermore. When there is life there will always be hope for all of us.

God has promised to make a way out of all of our battles. God will answer all of our prayers. In God's Perfect and Incredible Timing. God will make your difficult problems more manageable and bearable for you to cope with. God is the solution to all of your problems. God will make your spirit wholesome complete well rounded transformed enlightened insightful inspired empowered joyful peaceful happy forever and ever. Your worst and bad problems you experience are there to teach you. About God's important valuable greatest lessons that God wants you to learn. God will give you God's grace mercy love compassion. To stay strong courageous resilient brave.

Through all of your difficult hardships you experience. The void that you are missing in yourself. Is the place where God dwells within your spirit. Through the power of the holy spirit. God will make your spirit completely wholesome and fully centered in the power of the holy spirit. Where God dwells within your whole spirit totally. Your pain suffering struggles difficulties challenges you experience. Will strengthen you and make you courageous resilient disciplined ambitious driven. The more positive joyful peaceful happy loving forgiving you become. The more success you will have at conquering your painful problems. God will forever and always be there for you to conquer all of your most challenging problems. Always reach out to God for God's supernatural intervention.

God is always there to help support guide encourage love bless reward strengthen exalt your soul. Through your hardships trials troubles burdens upsets hurts. You go through in your life. God is always standing strongly and powerfully by your side through it all. God will bless you and reward you when you reach out to God for his special knowledge. God loves to bless and reward God's Precious Children. God's Perfect Love will take away all of your fears anxieties concerns insecurities uncertainties doubts. You are always in the capable hands of God.

You will meet God on Judgement Day when God calls you Home to be with God in Heaven. The closer you grow to God the closer God will grow to you. God loves you and adores you abundantly. God is your Rock through everything. God loves you so very much that God wants to take everything out of your life. That you have been struggling with and suffering with. When life is getting you down when you feel like life is unfair. Trust that God will turn everything around into your own favour. Jesus Christ Almighty took on all of your sicknesses addictions diseases brokeness illness pain suffering onto the cross.

By healing and saving you completely. Everyone hurts other people it is apart of being a human being. Always forgive be kind good loving to people who hurt you badly. God will make you fearless unfraid care free unattached. From your battles sickness addictions heartache pain grief. God will give you the victory power courage strength for you to be triumphant through it all. When you always choose to do the right thing. By being positive loving kind good fair just to everyone. Then God will always bless you and reward you big time in your life. God is renewing changing transforming making you stronger fixing you through your difficult problems.

When people forsake you and abandon you. Know that God will always be with you. God will comfort help love guide bless reward fulfill sustain encourage support you abundantly. You learn a lot more about God's Special Knowledge. Through going through your greatest pain and suffering. Your suffering you go through on Earth will make you wealthy in Heaven. Always rise above the knock backs that people can put you through. Place all of your faith love hope in God. God will make you victorious triumphant powerful through it all.

God will bless you in times of struggle. God will make you strong in times of weakness. God will exalt your spirits in times of despair. Everyone has been struggling with some long lived problem sickness addiction heartache difficulty pain grief. Your battles will strengthen you and you will grow more powerfully with your faith love hope in God. God will make you victorious triumphant powerful strong willed courageous enlightened positive empowered loving kind good forgiving fair just joyful peaceful happy truthful forevermore.

God will comfort you in times of sorrow. God will love you when you are hurting. God will reward you in times of sadness. God will support you in times of heartache. God knows all of the cries of your heart. God will make possible for you to conquer what you are find impossible to conquer. Pray by asking God for what you need. God will grant you the desires of your heart. Ask and you shall receive. Seek and you shall find. When there is a will there will always be a way. When you help yourself God will bless you and reward you abundantly. God blesses those people who help themselves. God will always be there to help bless reward glorify save set you totally free from everything.

God will keep you safe in God's warm open loving embracing arms forevermore. On Earth and in The Paradise of Heaven for all of Eternity. If you love yourself then other people will love you. If you don't love yourself then other people won't love you. God has got big plans to prosper bless fulfill reward direct your path into God's Powerful Love Wisdom Honour Glory. Never allow anyone to interfere with your spirits in negative and disempowering ways. God will love you protect you build you up keep you safe accept you.

God will always keep you strong willed enlightened empowered exalted through all of your challenging difficulties. God has got all of the power strength courage to make you feel better in everything you go through in your life. God will build you up in times of sorrow. God will bless you in times of despair. God will heal you in times of hurt. God knows so well what you are going through with your deepest and hardest sorrows struggles addictions battles sickness brokeness illness pain suffering. God will step in into your life by being there for you to heal fix save mend restore cleanse rectify you. God will make everything better for you always and forevemore.

Always love forgive be kind good to people who do you wrong. Pray a lovely and beautiful prayer for those people who are cruel to you. God will help you in times of trouble. God will encourage you when you are down. God will strengthen you in times of weakness. God will uplift your spirits when you feel helpless. The calmer more positive peaceful joyful happy content smart kinder caring good loving you become. The more you will succeed in conquering your problems. Sometimes people can project their cruel unkind mean nasty insincere feelings onto you. Don't take any notice of this kind of behaviour from people. God absolutely loves you and cherishes you unconditionally. Turn to God always God will never hurt you. God has promised to always and forever to be there for you.

Always find your identity in The Lord Jesus Christ Almighty. Don't find your identity in people. God will always and forever save you from your sins. God will reveal to you everything you need to know. Through the power of the holy spirit. God has made each of us uniquely. God has given each of us God's Special Knowledge that God has chosen for each of us. All of us need to learn to always be loving forgiving faithful devoted committed genuine sincere honest trustworthy. To maintain and to keep long term relationships.

God will open up the right and best opportunities and possibilities. For you in God's Perfect and Amazing Timing. Your difficult problems sickness addictions sadness anxiety grievances. Are your way to God. God will reveal Gods Powerful Truths and Laws to you. Through the power of the holy spirit. Everyone struggles with and suffers with some emotional problems or physical problems in their lives. God will cleanse purify rectify heal restore bless sanctify reward prosper you completely. From everything that is wrong with your health emotionally physically spiritually mentally. God is always there for you. To fix everything that is wrong with you.

Always be comfortable being uncomfortable. God will give you strength courage determination motivation discipline resilience ambition drive. God will always and forever make you fearless and unafraid through everything you will ever experience. God will make you Rich Full of God's goodness kindness love compassion sympathy empathy forgiveness always and forevermore. God loves you more than you can ever imagine. God will always bless you and reward you abundantly. Throughout all of your days on this Earth. From the beginning and until the end of your time on this Earth. God will be with you forever and ever. On Earth and in The Kingdom of Heaven for all of Eternity.

When you walk closely and securely with God. God will reveal to you God's Special Knowledge Truths Insights Laws Revelations always and forevermore. God is always and forever with you even at your darkest moments. God will inspire exalt enliven enrich empower enlighten bless love reward heal restore your soul always and forevermore. God will comfort sooth make you holy righteous pure innocent gracious clean dignified uplifted respectful unconditionally loving forgiving kind good just. When you are always with the right people who treat you well with respect consideration fairness. God will bless you and reward you big time.

God won't bless you and reward you if you are with the wrong people. God will love you when people hurt you. God will comfort you when people don't understand you. God will heal you when you are hurting. There is nothing that God can't do. God can and God will answer all of your prayers in God's Perfect and Outstanding Timing always and forevermore. God will always bring out the best in you and uplift your spirits in times of despair. God will inspire empower enlighten build you up restore replenish exalt your spirits always and forever and ever. God will always provide for you all of your needs desires wishes wants yearnings longings of your heart always and forevermore.

The truth of God will set you totally free from all of your sins. God loves you and adores you more than you can ever imagine. God will exalt your spirits when people are mean to you. God will love you when people reject you. God will help you when you are hurting. God will give you courage when people disappoint you. God will give you hope when you are down hearted. God will always save your soul through everything you will ever go through in your life. God's love for you will never fail you. God's love for you in Completely

Perfect Truthful Faithful Devoted Committed Loyal Righteous Holy Majestic Magnificent. On Earth and in The Paradise of Heaven for all of Eternity.

Always be respectful to disrespectful people. Be kind to unkind people. Be loving to unloving people. Be fair to unfair people. Be just to unjust people. You will make it through very well in your life. When you always have a strong consistent powerful faith love hope in God. God will take your spirit to The Paradise of Heaven in God's Perfect and Amazing Timing. Where you will dwell in Heaven with God for all of Eternity. God is closest most powerful strongest prominent to you. Through the hurt that people put you through and through your painful problems.

If you never give up you will always win. God will conquer all of your impossible problems addictions battles sicknesses brokeness heartaches pain suffering grievances. God is always with you when people mistreat you unfairly. God will comfort you in times of distress. God will make you feel better when you are hurting. When people hurt you let you down disappoint you. Trust that God will sustain heal restore prosper deliver save Glorify your soul always and forevermore. God will save you from your sins. God will rectify prosper redeem cure heal cleanse love forgive deliver your soul from everything.

Always hold tight to your Magnificent Faithful Holy Righteous Father God in Heaven. Then Father God will holy tight to you.

Nothing is impossible to God. God will answer all of your prayers. In God's Perfect and Outstanding Timing. God will save you and set you totally free from everything. God will find a way out of your impossible problems addictions battles sickness brokeness illness disease heartache hurt upset. God will make it possible for you to conquer all of your difficult problems. With God you have won all of the Victory Wisdom Honour Glory. To win surpass overcome conquer achieve accomplish all of your challenges. God will never let you go. God will hold you close to him always and forevermore.

God will bring to you great and amazing people who have a close relationship with God. Who will become your lifelong friends. God will heal deliver rescue save set you totally free from all of your insecurities anxieties doubts uncertainties fears depression always and forevermore. Everyone has got problems that they are caught in and stagnated in. That they can't escape from. Trust that God has got all of the power strength courage to save deliver restore rescue set you totally free from all of your difficult problems. That you have been suffering with.

God understands so well everything that troubles you and burdens you. God will make your burdens lighter for you to carry. God will resolve all of your difficulties. God works the most powerful and strongest through your pain and suffering. God will reveal to you God's Special Knowledge through your problems. Always have a positive strong steady faith love hope in God. God will see you through all of your trials and tribulations very well. God will give you hope when you feel hopeless. God will exalt your spirits when you are suffering. God will bless you and love you endlessly. On Earth and in The Kingdom of Heaven for all of Eternity. God will comfort you in times of despair.

God will give you peace when you are troubled. God will make you triumphant through everything. God will teach you all of your important lessons you need to learn. When you go through your worst experiences. Everyone is stuck in a rut with some impossible problems addictions battles sickness illness heartaches pain suffering grievances. Trust that God will eventually set you totally free by saving you. In The Paradise of Heaven there will be no more pain no more depression no more suffering no more sickness no more sorrow no more despair no more grief. God will make your spirit completely perfect sublime surreal peaceful joyful blissful tranquil happy healthy excited forever to come forevermore. On Earth and in The Kingdom of Heaven for all of Eternity.

God will help you to overcome and conquer all of your painful problems. That you have been struggling with for decades and decades. With God everything will always be possible. Our problems are our source of strength that drives us to be closer deeper richer in our faith love hope in God. Always have friends who treat you well. Who you know you can trust. Who never hurt you unfairly. Pray for people who don't appreciate you. God will help you when you feel low spirited. God will always give you courage when you need it the most.

The power of God's love will move your heart to a better place. Your faith love hope in God will save you through everything. God will make all of your problems to work out for the best. With your consistent faith love hope in God. God will make you happy. God will provide for you all of your needs and desires of your heart. When you choose to make wise choices and decisions in your life. God will reign down with God's rich full wholesome blessings rewards delights surprises into your life. God has given you painful problems for you to understand. And for you to grow deeper closer stronger more powerfully to God yourself and other people.

God wants you to put God first above everyone on this Earth. Your relationship with God. Is the most important relationship you will ever have on Earth and in The Paradise of Heaven for all of Eternity. God will make you Almighty Victorious Triumphant Compassionate Sympathetic Empathetic Unconditionally Loving Forgiving Patient Kind Hearted Good Willed always and forevermore. With God you will always conquer by winning all of your trials and tribulations. God will give you all of the positivity strength hope courage you need to survive really well in your life. God is always there for you to count on through everything you will ever experience in your life. God will never let you down disappoint you. God loves you and treasures you more than anything.

You can always put your complete faith love hope in God. God will never disappoint you. God always has your best interests within God's heart. When a friend rejects you. Trust that God will guide you to other great and amazing people. Who will be better friends. Always have friends who make you joyful peaceful happy. Who respect you and enjoy your company. God's love for you is indescribable and unbelievable. God's love for you will bring you total freedom liberation positivity independence into your life. God's love for you will last forevermore. On Earth and in The Paradise of Heaven for all of Eternity.

God will give you a Perfect Healthy Heavenly Spiritual Pure spirit. In The Paradise of Heaven for all of Eternity. Everything we say is a reflection of how we feel within ourselves. Happiness always comes from within ourselves. God wants to pour out God's blessings rewards delights surprises unconditional love kindness goodness integrity respect wholeness onto you. The closer stronger deeper richer more powerful your faith love hope becomes in God. You will see how God will move mountains for you in your life. Like you could of never imagined possible. Each of us are responsible and accountable for our own emotions.

Never blame or be disrespectful nasty mean towards anyone. Always be respectful considerate positive loving kind good fair just to everyone. When people are against you. Know in your heart that God is always for you. God is perfecting your ways through your trials. Your help support guidance encouragement inspiration insights. Always comes from your Lord Jesus Christ Almighty. From the power of the holy spirit from God. God will cleanse purity sustain sanctify replenish fix prosper nourish bless fulfill reward empower enlighten Save your soul always and forevermore. God is always and forever with you through all of your challenges. God will make you improve and get better in every great way. In everything you do.

Through your painful problems God is working through you the most. To teach guide comfort heal help reasurre rectify love you endlessly always and forevermore. God will always and forever make you rich full of God's goodness kindness grace mercy respect dignity joy peace happiness enless love fairness compassion forgiveness wisdom honour Glory. When you work hard at developing a close strong powerful faith love hope in God. Your problems battles addictions sickness pain suffering grief. Will fade away more and more every day.

When you are down hearted God will build you up. When you feel in despair God will love you. When you have sorrow God will comfort you. God will love you endlessly when you are troubled. God will make you positive when you are feeling down. God will make you powerful in times of distress. God will open up the right doors for you to develop meaningful rewarding insightful truthful friendships. Who will have close strong deep powerful relatiohships with God. With people who will always love you. For the person you are. When you are down with problems. God will turn your life around for the best.

God will bless you and reward you with God's joy peace happiness love hope excitement compassion forgiveness always and forevermore.

When there is life there will always be hope for all of us. God will make a way out of your problems. God will answer all of your prayers. God can do everything for you that you can't do yourself. God has got all of the power strength courage to heal you from everything. God will bless you through sickness and health. God will heal deliver save set you totally free. From your heartache pain brokeness sickness struggles suffering hurts upsets grievances. With God you will feel a lot better within your spirits.

What you struggle with and suffer with the most will draw you closer stronger deeper powerful to God. God will heal save set you totally free from everything. Always be with people who you know are worthy and deserving of your time. Don't be with people that you can't trust. God will bless you and reward you with God's supernatural truths insights laws revelations. And God's special knowledge for all of Eternity. God will always bless cherish treasure reward value adore appreciate be kind fair good love you endlessly forevermore.

God will heal save set you totally free unleash all of your chains from your sins brokenness sicknesses addictions despairs sorrows. God has got all of the solutions to all of your problems. God will make a way out of your mess. When you feel like there is no way out. God will comfort you in times of despair. God will bless you in times of sorrow. God will uplift your spirits in times of sadness. God will answer all of your prayers. In God's Perfect and Amazing Timing. God will bring you peace joy hope love compassion happiness to your spirit forever and ever. With God's help you can accomplish everything.

Always be with positive and empowering people who uplift your spirits and who bring out the best in you. When people hurt you deeply understand that they are dealing with their own troubles burdens hurts upsets sadness despairs sorrows. God knows so well everything you are struggling with and suffering with. God will make you victorious triumphant powerful through it all. Persevere persist be patient through your impossible battles addictions sicknesses diseases heartache pain suffering grievances. God will deliver you totally from all of your problems. Always stick with people who treat you right. Who are always respectful considerate polite courteous kind hearted good willed fair just towards you.

Sometimes God allows us to struggle with and suffer with painful problems. For us to open up our hearts and souls to God's special knowledge. Through the power of the holy spirit from God. Stay strong resilient polite respectful kind good loving fair just courageous forgiving. To people in this world who try to knock you down. Always find your identity in your Lord Jesus Christ Almighty. Don't find your identity in people. You grow closer stronger deeper powerful in your faith love hope in God. When people hurt you badly. Always forgive and love every person who hurts you.

God understands you the best better than any person knows you. God is always there to help bless guide protect lead build you up always and forevermore. God will make you victorious triumphant powerful through everything. Never hurt anyone emotionally. Always have unconditional endless love kindness goodness respect integrity grace mercy compassion forgiveness towards everyone. All of us need to learn to always treat each other with respect trust consideration kindness goodness love compassion fairness justness. With God you have got everything. God will make a way out of all of your impossible problems addictions sicknesses depression anxiety hurts upsets grievances.

When you respect people by doing positive kind loving good fair just deeds. God will bless you and reward you big time. God will give you all of the answers to your problems you are looking for in your life. God's love for you is perfect sublime surreal pure innocent righteous divine holy supreme majestic magnificent beautiful. Your suffering will make your faith love hope in God more prominent and powerful. With faith and trust in God everything can be achieved overcome conquered surpassed accomplished always and forevermore. The closer you become to God the closer God will become to you. God is always there for you no matter what you are going through in your life.

Religious Quotes Book 2

od will turn everything around for good. By making everything better for you. Through God's love blessings rewards good fortune. God will make possible what you are finding impossible to conquer. God will give you all of the victory power success. You are looking for. God will give you strength when you feel hopeless. God will give you courage when people are mean to you. God will heal your soul completely. God will uplift your spirits when you are down. God will heal all of your wounds. God will reward you when people don't accept you. With God you will be triumphant in all things.

God's love will make you victorious. God's healing powers will restore you. God will bless you and reward you. With God's Special Knowledge through your difficulties. God will always and forever save and Glorify your soul. God is always for you when people are against you. God always loves you when people are cruel to you. God will exalt your spirits. When people are mean nasty spiteful towards you. Pray a loving forgiving kind good lovely beautiful prayer for them. With God all things are possible. God loves you beyond your comprehension. God will love you forever and ever.

God will give you inspiration when your life has no meaning. God will give you hope when you feel helpless. God will sustain you. Be with people who can see your positivity love beauty goodness. God will uplift your spirits when you are down. God will heal all of your wounds. God will reward you when people don't accept you. God will take away your suffering. God will give you hope when you are burdened. God will remove your troubles. God will remove from you all of your battles. Through the great love mercy grace compassion forgiveness. God has got for you. Your faith love hope you have in God. Will see you through all of your challenging obstacles. You will ever experience in your life.

God will always bless you and reward you. With God's peace excitement joy satisfaction delightfulment happiness always and forevermore. God will grant you all of your deepest desires of your heart. God loves to bless and reward God's Precious Children. Always walk closely with God and God will always walk closely with you. God is our source of peace health joy contentment happiness love compassion forgiveness hope prosperity. God will conquer all of your challenging problems. Through God's pure grace mercy compassion love. God has got for you. God is always there for you amongst your heartache pain grief.

God will bless you and love you. By making you feel a lot better. You can't always rely on people. God wants you to rely completely on God. With all of your heart and soul. Then you will be happy. God will save your soul through it all. God absolutely loves you and adores you. God will remove all of your battles from you. God knows your needs and desires before you do. God will grant you all of your needs and desires of your heart always and forevermore. God knows the conflict heartache pain grief. That you go through in your relationships. God will always make you feel a lot better.

God will bless you and reward you with God's peace joy happiness love excitement compassion. Through your trials troubles burdens tribulations. Our suffering makes our faith love hope in God. More stronger richer deeper closer powerful. When you always live in God's Unconditional love. God will take away all of your fears anxieties doubts insecurities uncertainties. God's Unconditional love respect compassion kindness goodness forgiveness. Is infinitely more powerful than your battles. God has got all of the power strength courage. To heal you completely from everything you have been battling with throughout your whole life.

God will heal rectify save deliver help support encourage you. To overcome conquer surpass accomplish everything. You have ever wanted to conquer in your life. God will bless you when people reject you. God will heal you when you are hurting. God will always reward you and love you through it all. God will give you the helping hand you need. To be strong courageous confident. God will make you triumphant through everything. God's love grace mercy holiness care. God has got for you. Will take away all of your fear anxiety concern doubt hurt within you.

Your relationship with God is the most important relationship you will ever have. Always depend on God no matter what. The only thing that matters in the end. Is that you have got a secure strong firm steady faith in God. Throughout all of your whole life. There is absolutely no problem that you have. That God can't conquer. God will give you all of the power strength courage. For you to be victorious through it all. God knows you a lot better than anyone knows you. God will heal restore deliver save replenish set you totally free from everything. God will make you stand strong.

When people try to tear you down. God will exalt your spirits through your most testing times. God will solve all of your problems. God will wash away your most challenging problems. With God's Great Love and Laws. God has got for you. God wants to make you truly lucky blessed fortunate privileged. In every great way. God especially blesses and rewards God's believers. God knows so well how it can hurt so much. When people don't accept agree reject the things you say and believe in. God will love you when you are hurting. God will save you from your sins. God will exalt your spirits when you are down. God will always be there for you to guide lead bless reward help support encourage love make you happy.

God has allowed people to disappoint us. So we can focus our full attention on God. God is the most important reason why we exist. With God there is always positivity hope for a better brighter truthful blessed rewarding future. God will wash away all of your sorrow. God will exalt your spirits when you are sad. God is always there for you through it all. God will make you victorious triumphant powerful through it all. God will heal cure deliver rectify save set you totally free. From all of your battles. Everyone is an individual. All of us need to respect each other with our differences.

By never being critical and judgemental towards anyone. God is always there for you amongst your heartache pain grief. God will bless you and reward you and love you. By making you feel better. God will do everything you can't do. God will give you the helping hand you need. To be strong courageous confident. God will make you triumphant through it all. God will bless you when people reject you. God will heal you when you are hurting. God will always bless you and reward you and love you forever and ever. God knows your needs and desires before you do.

God will grant you all of your needs and desires of your heart forevermore. God will conquer all of your challenging problems. Through God's pure grace mercy compassion love forgiveness. God has got for you. When you have got the endless love of God within your heart and soul. God will bless you and reward you. With God's love grace mercy hope gratitude. There is power through the holy spirit where God dwells within your soul. God will miraculously heal cleanse save Glorify your soul forever and ever. God will do everything for you that you can't do. Through God's strength grace mercy love power help support. God has got for you. God will always stand by you through everything you will ever go through in your life.

You learn grow stronger the most through your most challenging battles. God will make you victorious through everything. We need to go through trials to become closer to God. Our painful problems help us to believe in God ourselves and each other more powerfully. When life gets you down. Hold onto your faith love hope in God. God will prosper help heal save support fulfill sustain your soul. When you are troubled with your burdens. Know that you have got a Glorious Righteous Faithful Loving Father God in Heaven who loves you and appreciates you tremendously.

God will make you strong when you are weak. God will make you happy when you are sad. God will go on loving you forever and ever. God has got great and amazing people for you to meet. Who will have a close relationship with God. Who will become your lifelong friends. Throughout all of our lives. God will continuously keep on loving and forgiving us from all of the mistakes we make. It is important for all of us to learn from all of the mistakes we make. God loves you more than anything. God will bless love forgive prosper reward help encourage support you through everything always and forevermore.

When you always believe in God then God will always believe in you. God teaches you the most through your most difficult problems. God has God's ways of working everything out for the best. For those people who believe in honour love worship our Father God in The Kingdom of Heaven. God will make possible for you to conquer your impossible problems. Your impossible problems are your way to God. Some people want to see you win by succeeding. Some other people want to see you lose by not succeeding. Don't let anyone ever stop you succeeding with achieving your goals ambitions dreams. Always believe in yourself. Always have a steady firm secure faith in God.

Have your own beliefs values attributes qualities. Don't follow the crowd. Be an individual with your own characteristics. God always has his ways of working everything out for the best in your favour. Through your most challenging problems. Never give up on God then God will never give up on you. God will find a way out of your most difficult problems. Until you find complete victory and triumph through all of your trials. God will give you everything you need and desire for in your life. God will bless prosper reward fulfil satisfy delight you always and forevermore. God will make things happen for you in your life.

God will give your life purpose meaning truth mission. God will never leave you on your own. God will always and forever be with you. You grow learn advance become stronger wiser better resilient disciplined. Through going through your most painful problems. When people reject you badly. Trust that God will bring into your life better people who will never reject you. When you are feeling alone. Trust that God will provide you with all of the right friends. Who will keep you company. When you are feeling down in despair. Trust that your Faithful Righteous Loving Father God is always close to you loving you and blessing you.

God will comfort you in times of sadness. God will help you when you feel helpless. God will always love you and bless you. God will always be there for you. When people turn against you. God will save you and set you totally free through it all. God will pick your spirits up when you feel down. God will love you always. God will exalt your spirits through everything. God loves beyond your comprehension. God loves you beyond your understanding. God loves you more than you can fathom. God will bring to you the best people. Who have a close relationship with God. Who will become your lifelong friends. God will comfort you in times of hurt. God will always hold you close.

God will build up your spirits in times of sorrow. God will always bless you and love your soul forever. With God there is always positivity hope for a better brighter truthful blessed rewarding future. When you feel low spirited trust that God will make you feel better. God will bless you and reward you with security joy peace happiness. God will love you when people don't value you. God will bless you when people don't relate to you. God will always be there to love you and reward you abundantly. God will give you strength when you feel hopeless. With God everything will always be fine.

God will give you courage when people are mean to you. God will heal your soul always and forevermore. God will heal your broken relationships. God will restore you when you feel hopeless. God will grant you all of your desires. The only thing in the end that you can always depend on the most. Is God's Everlasting Eternal faith love hope you have in God. God will take away your suffering. God will give you hope when you are burdened. God will remove your troubles. Through God's miraculous healing powers. God will bless you with excellent health spiritually emotionally physically mentally. God will intervene into your life. By healing delivering curing saving blessing rewarding rescuing setting you totally free from all of your difficulties.

With God you can conquer everything that is troubling you and burdening you. God will make you victorious through everything. When people don't accept you pray for them. When people reject you forgive them. When people hurt you unfairly love them. God will guide you to the best people. Who will always treat you well with respect kindness goodness fairness love. In God's Perfect and Amazing Timing. God will completely deliver heal restore rescue help save set you totally free from everything. God will always and forever give you everything you are looking for in your life. God always wants to make you completely fulfilled delighted satisfied happy forever and ever. From the beginning and until the end of time on this Earth.

Over time your painful problems will become easier more manageable and bearable for you to cope with. Nothing ever is impossible to God. With God all things will always be possible to accomplish. Always be with people who make you feel good uplifted accepted valued appreciated understood cherished treasured. God will bless you with positivity independence freedom. The more kind loving good deeds you do for other people. God allows us to suffer with our painful problems. So we can grow more strongly deeply closely powerfully. With our faith in God.

God will make you Almighty Courageous Strong Compassionate Forgiving Loving Kind Good Fair Just always and forevermore. Not everyone will like you in this world and that's okay. Be with people who always accept value appreciate love cherish treasure you completely. God will conquer your impossible battles Victoriously Triumphantly Powerfully. Until the end of your time on this Earth. Love people who mistreat you unfairly. Pray a kind prayer for people who do you wrong. Forgive and love people who are mean to you. God will forever and always make you fruitful blessed joyful peaceful happy healthy wise loving kind just forever and ever. You can overcome conquer achieve surpass. Be Victorious Triumphant Powerful. By always having faith love hope in God.

In The Paradise of Heaven with God everyone everything everywhere. Will be Perfect Tranquil Blissful Harmonious Peaceful Magnificent Majestic Serene Surreal Beautiful Lovely always and forevermore. God will always make you Victorious Triumphant Powerful. Through your trials troubles burdens tribulations. Your unfair difficult problems that you find impossible to conquer. Are your way to God. God will always help you when you feel helpless. God will make you

Triumphant through all of your difficult battles. With the great love goodness kindness grace mercy compassion forgiveness fairness. That God has got for you forever and ever.

When people hurt you by letting you down. Trust that you have got a Glorious Righteous Faithful Loving Father God Almighty. Who absolutely loves you and treasures you completely. You are very important to God. God will give you the strength tenacity endurance for you to keep on going in your life. Never ever give up. God will always make your life a lot better. If you never ever give up. Then you will always win all of your challenges. Keep on persevering persisting and being patient and you will make it through everything.

All of us are a gift and a blessing from God. God loves you more than you can ever imagine. God will go on loving you forever and ever. On Earth and in The Paradise of Heaven always and forevermore. The difficult things in your life that are holding you back. Will strengthen your faith in God. By giving you positivity and hope. God will heal bless prosper reward all of your relationships. God loves to bless and reward God's Precious Children. God will correct for you everything that has been going wrong for you. God will save you by setting you totally free from your trials. God will hold you close to God. When people don't show you empathy. God will love you when people hurt you. God will always love bless reward you always and forever.

There is light at the end of every tunnel. Every grey cloud has got a silver lining. When there is a will there will always be a way. When there is life there will always be hope for all of us. God will reveal everything you need to know through the power of the holy spirit from God. God will bless you and reward you. With joy peace happiness hope love positivity excitement truth. Through your trials hurts upsets tribulations. God will bless prosper reward fulfil sustain exalt love forgive build you up Glorify your soul always and forevermore. God will make your spirit Perfect in God's Image. In The Paradise of Heaven for all of Eternity. God will give you all of the positivity hope courage you need to keep on living well in your life.

God will save you from your sins. Always live in God's truths and laws. Then God will bless you and reward you big time. God's love takes away all fear anxiety doubt uncertainty insecurity hurt upset heartache grief always and forevermore. God will bless you and reward you. With excellent health emotionally spiritually physically mentally always and forevermore. In The Paradise of Heaven there will be no more pain no more suffering no more sickness no more heartache no more depression no more despair no more sorrow no more grief. God will deliver you completely from all of your impossible battles in Heaven. Where none of your battles will ever exist anymore.

God will make your spirit in Heaven completely Perfect in God's Image forever to come forevermore. God will give you the positivity hope good health courage kind hearted good willed forgiving nature. For you to always be healthy and happy. God will always cleanse sanctify heal save deliver purify stabilize bless. Your heart mind body spirit soul forever and ever. God will always keep you sane together well grounded peaceful joyful happy healthy forgiving loving kind good fair just forevermore. Those people who endure to the end with their faith love hope in God will be saved. God will grant all of your desires of your heart.

In God's Perfect and Majestic Timing. God loves you and adores you more than anything. God will perform God's miraculous blessings rewards delights surprises. To heal you totally from your sicknesses troubles diseases illnesses burdens hurts upsets grievances. Hallelujah Praise The Lord Jesus Christ Almighty. On Earth and in The Kingdom of Heaven for all of Eternity. One day in God's Perfect Timing. God will reveal to you why things in your life happened to you. The way they did. God will ask you on judgement day how did you help other people. God will solve all of your problems forever.

God knows you better than anyone else knows you. God knows you better than you know yourself. When you are always loving kind forgiving to people who hurt you unfairly. You will never go wrong. When God closes one door in your life. Then God will open up better more amazing blessed fulfilling rewarding doors in your life. God will comfort you when people don't appreciate you. God will love you when people reject you. God will always bless you love you reward you. When people don't love you properly respect them. When people insult you love and forgive them. Love everyone always. It is in the stillness that God reveals himself to you.

God wants you to seek him above everyone and everything. Be respectful to disrespectful people. Be kind to unkind people. Be fair to unfair people. Be loving to unloving people. God will help you to conquer all of your impossible problems. In God's Perfect and Majestic Timing. Your painful problems are your way to God. God tests you then rewards you. Always be faithful to God. Then God will always be faithful to you. In God's Perfect and Amazing Timing. God will deliver and set you totally free from your most difficult problems addictions battles. God will heal save rescue deliver unleash all of your chains set you totally free. From your sicknesses diseases illnesses addictions heartaches pain suffering grievances.

God will turn your bad problems around into the most beautiful brilliant amazing incredible blessings rewards for your own favour always and forevermore. When people let you down disappoint you hurt you. Know that your Father God has plans to prosper bless fulfil inspire you always and forevermore. God will comfort you when people don't appreciate you. God will love you when people reject you. God will always bless you love you reward you always and forevermore. With God by your side you will never go wrong. God is the answer to all of your problems. God has got a lot of love for you. God's love for you will conquer all of your battles.

God will give your life meaning truths insights laws revelations purpose. God will make missions for you to accomplish in your life. God will love you when you are hurting. God will exalt your spirits through everything always and forevermore. Always build people up never tear anyone down. Always uplift people's spirits by bringing out the best in everyone. God knows so well everything you struggle with in your life. Time heals all of your wounds. God will always make you feel better. God will renew replenish exalt uplift bless reward prosper comfort reassure help guide love you endlessly for all of Eternity.

Your most challenging problems are your way to God. Your faith in God is more powerful than your battles. God will make you victorious and triumphant in all things. God is your Comforter Healer Redeemer Exalter Uplifter Deliverer Saviour Helper Transformer Life Line through everything you will ever experience in your life. When you feel burdened with troubles. Open up your heart and soul to God. God will always comfort you by making you feel better and happy within yourself. God will always strengthen exalt empower fulfil sustain build you up and Glorify your soul. Through your pain and suffering. God will amaze inspire move bless enlighten empower support guide love forgive save your soul through it all always and forever and ever.

God will make you blessed fortunate lucky privileged. On Earth and in The Paradise of Heaven for all of Eternity. Your impossible battles will teach you all about God's truths laws promises. Never hurt anyone unfairly. Always be respectful positive kind good loving fair just to everyone. God will bless you big time. When you are always with the right people. God won't bless you at all if you are with the wrong people. Always be with people who respect you and love you for the person you are. Who you know you can trust and confide in completely.

Don't waste your time with people who are negative and toxic. Always be with people who build you up. Who treat you well right fair. Your impossible battles will make you thrive nourish flourish blossom bloom in your faith in God. The power of the holy spirit from God that is within you. God will heal you from all of your battles. Not everyone is going to like you in this world and that's okay. Always be with people who love you and adore you completely. Count all of your blessings. Look at everything that God has done for you. Always be grateful thankful appreciative for everything God has given you. Always build people up never tear anyone down.

Always uplift people's spirits by bringing out the best in everyone. Always be with positive and empowering people. Stay away from negative and disempowering people. Always be with people who treat you well right just. Remove yourself away from people who treat you wrong not right unjust. God will move mountains for you in your life. God will do the impossible for you. That you could never of imagined possible. God will answer all of your prayers. In God's Perfect and Majestic Timing. When you always stay close to God. Then God will always stay close to you. Always have strong certain secure faith love hope in God. God will always turn around everything into good.

From God's unconditional love God has got for you. Always have a strong courageous tolerant resilient love forgiveness compassion.

Towards people who mistreat you unfairly. God will bless you and reward you. With God's peace joy happiness grace compassion empathy mercy forgiveness. Through all of your battles always and forevermore. God will always make your spirits calm settled tranquil blissful sane together restful relaxed blessed happy go lucky forevermore. God will fix you by making it possible for you to conquer all of your. Impossible problems addictions pain hurts suffering upsets. God will go on loving you always and forevermore. With God you will always have everything you will ever need.

Always be with the right people. Who love you and accept you for who you are. Who like and enjoy your company. The difficult things in your life that are holding you back. Will strengthen your faith in God. By giving you positivity and hope for a better brighter more productive rewarding fulfilling blessed fruitful future. No matter how much you feel powerless in conquering. Your problems addictions sicknesses diseases heartache pain grief. Trust that God will set you totally free always and forevermore. God will bring into your life the right people. Who will be respectful kind good accepting loving forgiving fair just truthful to you. God loves to bless and reward God's Precious Children.

From God's pure righteous holy gracious merciful love. God has got for you always and forever and ever. With faith and trust in God everything can be achieved overcome conquered surpassed accomplished. If you never give up then you will always win all of your battles. Never lose hope. God will make your life a whole lot better. God will exalt your spirits when you are down hearted. God will help you when you are sad. God will love you when you are hurting. God will make you strong when you are weak. Stable when you are unstable. Peaceful when you are uptight.

Calm when you are anxious. Don't let anyone crush your spirits. Always build people up. Bring out the best in people. Uplift people's spirits always and forevermore. When life gets you down. How people can disappoint by letting you down. Trust that God has got an amazing meaningful exciting rewarding future ahead for you. With God you can always be peaceful joyful happy hopeful positive respectful forgiving sympathetic empathetic always and forevermore. God will make you Positive when you are negative. Secure when you are insecure. Certain when you are uncertain. Clear headed when you are doubtful. Strong when you are weak. Thoughtful when you are struggling within yourself. Happy when you are sad always.

God will heal deliver rescue save set you totally free. From all of your impossible battles always and forevermore. One day in God's Perfect and Amazing Timing. God will make it possible for you to conquer your most challenging problems. Keep on persevering and persisting through your battles. In God's Perfect Timing. God will make you victorious through it all. People can't love you how God loves you. God's love is completely Perfect but our love as people is imperfect. Don't ever let anyone stop you succeeding your aspirations ambitions dreams. God's love for you is perfect righteous pure holy clean majestic magnificent kind good loving fair just completely.

You can't always rely on people. God will never let you down hurt you or disappoint you. God loves you beyond your comprehension always and forevermore. Never lose your faith in God. Never lose your faith in Heaven. Always have a close honest faithful truthful relationship with God. God will always turn around your negative and bad situations. Into positive and good situations. God will make you positive when you are negative. Happy when you are sad. Respectful when you are disrespectful. Grateful when you are ungrateful. Satisfied when you are unsatisfied. God will give you hope when you feel helpless in your burdens. God will inspire you when you feel lost.

God will always bless you love you reward you. From the beginning and until the end of your time on this Earth. God will bless love reward fulfil exalt forgive sustain heal restore replenish blossom set you totally free Glorify your soul forever and ever. You will never fail in your life. When you have a strong firm steady faith love hope in God always and forevermore. Without God you can't be peaceful joyful happy loving kind good fair just respectful forgiving. Always be with people who you can trust. Who have your best interests within their hearts. Who always treat you right well just. God will bless you and reward you when you are always with the right and best people. Who love you for who you are.

God is the source of your strength compassion grace mercy forgiveness gratitude endless love kindness goodness. God will shine God's beacon ray of light through your darkest moments. God will save you by setting you totally free from everything. God will bless fulfil sustain reward empower enlighten help guide support encourage you always and forevermore. Always find your identity in The Lord Jesus Christ Almighty. Don't find your identity in people. God will make your life exciting adventurous interesting meaningful truthful inspiring insightful fun-loving. God is always there for you.

God will comfort you in times of sadness. God will exalt your spirits in times of despair. God will always bless you love you reward you. God will make your spirit Perfect in God's Image in The Paradise of Heaven for all of Eternity forever to come forevermore. Don't let people who mistreat you unfairly get to you in the slightest. Love them and forgive them. You will get through this really well. God will turn your biggest weaknesses around into your greatest strengths. God will deliver you and heal you from everything. God will find a way out of your painful problems. Always pray for people who mistreat you unfairly. God is always right by your side through it all.

When people reject you in cruel ways. Pray for them. When people mistreat you unfairly. Always love them and forgive them. Always be courageous by having a strong resolve and a brave resilience. When people mistreat you unfairly. God allows us to get hurt by other people so we can grow richer stronger closer deeper more powerful. In our faith in God. When there is life there will always be hope for all of us. God has got great and amazing people who you are going to meet. Who will have a very close deep strong faithful relationship in God. God will amaze inspire move bless enlighten empower reward help support guide love forgive your soul always and forever and ever.

With God you will always be able to succeed in every area of your life always and forevermore. God will never let you down.

God will bless you and reward you with positivity independence freedom. The more kind loving good deeds you do for other people. Always have friends who treat you well in genuine sincere honest trustworthy ways. You become like the people you associate with the most. Choose your companion and friends very carefully and wisely. Nothing and no one can ever hurt you. When you have a strong firm steady faith love hope in God. God loves you more than anything. God's love for you will see you through all of your battles triumphantly. Always be thankful grateful appreciative for everything God has done and will ever do for you in your life. You will make it.

With God there will always be positivity and hope. For a fantastic joyful peaceful happy rewarding truthful blessed meaningful future. Be with the right people who you feel safe around. Who will never mistreat you unfairly. Who you know you can trust completely. God is teaching you your most important valuable greatest lessons. When you experience your most painful problems. Always be respectful considerate kind loving good positive fair just to everyone. Never mistreat anyone unfairly. God will heal sanctify cleanse restore rectify help support encourage reveal save set you totally free Glorify your soul always and forever and ever. God will always be there.

God works the most powerful through your greatest suffering. Your painful problems are teaching you all about God's Special Knowledge.

God will do everything for you that you can't do for yourself. God will remove your difficult battles. From God's love for you. You will make it through all of your battles. With your faith love hope in God. God will always make you victorious through it all. Don't spend your time worrying about anything. Always focus on everything God has rewarded you and blessed you with in your life. God blesses you according to the intentions of your heart. When you always live in God's truths and laws. God will bless you and reward you abundantly. God will always be with you to love you help you.

When you stop contacting toxic people. By always being with positive kind just people. You will always be blessed and happy. God will step into your life. God will conquer all of your most challenging problems. In God's Perfect and Amazing Timing. Your painful problems will make you stronger better closer richer healthier wiser well established. With your faith in God. God will give you the strength courage power. For you to overcome conquer surpass everything. When you are always with the right and best people. You will always flourish nourish blossom bloom through everything.

God will reward you when people don't like you. God will bless you when you are with the best people. Who are kind just to you. With a strong firm steady faith in God. God will help you to conquer all of your impossible battles. When people wound you badly with their unjust words. Always love and forgive them. Pour out your loving kind goodness to them. Forgive people who reject you. Love people who mistreat you unfairly. Pray for people who don't accept you. God loves you more than you can imagine. God's love is real just. God's love mercy grace compassion will heal you from your sicknesses battles trials. God will help you when you are lonely. When people disappoint you. Trust that God is always there for you.

Guiding loving blessing rewarding saving your soul. When people disappoint you and hurt you. Turn to your Glorious Father God in Heaven. God will give you peace and rest to your soul. God will bless you and reward you. With God's peace joy happiness love excitement compassion. Through all of your trials troubles burdens tribulations. Always bring out the beauty love positivity kindness goodness compassion respect in everyone. God will always and forever get you through all of your hardships. This is God's job. God will love you endlessly forevermore. When people don't accept you. Forgive them. When people are mean to you. Pray for them. God will always make you happy when you are sad. God will exalt your spirits through it all. God will help you through all of your problems.

God will brighten up your spirits completely. With God you can always accomplish everything. Always focus on God. Then God will always focus on you at all times. God will always bless you with a tranquil blissful surreal serene pure righteous holy peaceful positive truthful spirit forever and ever. Every relationship has its challenges. We have always lived in a fallen world. Ever since the Garden of Eden. None of us will be perfect on this Earth. As long as you always learn from your mistakes. You'll be fine. Don't ever let anyone get the better of you. Always be with people who are kind honest loving just. Who will never hurt you. Who you know you can trust and confide in completely. Always have friends who are close to God.

God knows all of your painful battles you have been going through. God will make everything in your life a lot better. God will open up your spirit more and more every day. For you to draw closer deeper stronger powerful. In your faith love hope in God. God's love is completely compassionate majestic divine righteous holy pure clean innocent forgiving just fair beautiful lovely forevermore. God has got all of the power and control over everyone on this Earth. God will take your spirit to Heaven. In God's Perfect and Majestic Timing. God will heal you from your burdens. God will bless you in times of your trials. God will support you in times of despair. God will reward you.

God will always love you when you are hurting. God is there for you always. God loves you more than you can imagine. God will help you to conquer all of your impossible battles victoriously. Always be with people who want to help you to succeed with your goals ambitions dreams. Who will always wish you well by wanting the best for you. God will always and forever bless love protect keep you safe comfort forgive help support encourage hold you close to God forever and ever. God will look after you through sickness and health. From the beginning and until the end of your time on this Earth. God is always helping you. God is always supporting you and guiding you. God will make your impossible battles possible for you to conquer. God will.

The more kind loving good deeds you do for other people. The more good luck good fortune success. God will bless you and reward you with forevermore. God will love you when people reject you. God will build you up when you are down. God will exalt your spirits when you are sad. God will deliver save set you totally free from your battles addictions sickness diseases grief. In God's Perfect and Amazing Timing. Your faith love hope in God will see you through all of your impossible battles triumphantly. Hold on God is going to get rid of all of your most challenging problems very soon. God is love.

If you never give up then you will always win. Keep on persevering persisting being patient through everything always. You will make it. God wants to bless you and reward you more than you can imagine. Always live in God's truths and laws. God loves you beyond your comprehension. Always be thankful grateful appreciative for everything God has done for you. And everything God has been doing for you in your life now. God loves to bless and reward. God's Precious Children. From God's pure righteous holy gracious merciful love God has got for you. With God all things are possible always. God will heal sanctify rectify cleanse purify restore replenish your health. Emotionally spiritually physically mentally always and forevermore. God will give you everything you are looking for.

Your painful problems teach you all about God's insights truths laws revelations. That God wants you to learn in your life. God will comfort you in times of despair. God will heal you in times of sorrow. God will make you strong when you are weak. God knows everything that burdens you and troubles you. God will make your life better joyful happier worthwhile truthful rewarding. God will melt and sooth you by giving you a soft strong loving compassionate empathetic sympathetic heart and soul. God will make your plans to turn out. The way they are meant to turn out. God always knows best. God will grant you all of the desires and needs of your heart.

Your pain and suffering will bring you. Closer deeper richer more real dignified graceful powerful. With your faith in God. God will heal cure deliver save unleash all of your chains set you totally free. From your illnesses diseases battles heartache pain suffering grief. There is the right reasons and right purposes and right ways. How every situation and circumstance will fall into place. The ways they are meant to. Always be with people who build you up who make you happy. Never be with people who tear you down by making you unhappy. God loves to bless and reward God's Precious Children.

Turn to God God will take away all of your worries. God absolutely loves you and adores you completely. With God everything is possible but without God everything is impossible. God has allowed people to disappoint us. So we can focus our full attention on God. God is the most important reason why we exist. Don't let anyone ever stop you succeeding your goals ambitions dreams. Always believe in yourself. By having a steady faith in God. God loves you. God will make it possible for you to conquer your impossible problems. Your impossible problems are your way to God. With a strong firm steady faith love hope in God. You will always be able to win in every area of your life successfully. God teaches you the most through your most difficult problems. God has his ways of working everything out for the best. When you always believe in God.

Then God will always believe in you. Throughout all of our lives. God will continuously keep on forgiving us and loving us. For all of the mistakes we make. From God's unconditional love kindness goodness compassion forgiveness gratitude thankfulness appreciation. That God has got for all of us. When life gets you down. Hold onto your faith love hope in God. God will prosper help heal save support fulfil sustain your soul through it all. We need to go through trials to become closer to God. Our painful problems help us to believe more powerfully. In God ourselves each other by always being faithful devoted committed with our faith love hope in God.

God will exalt your spirits in times of despair. God will comfort you in times of sorrow. God will always be there for you. You learn grow stronger the most through your most challenging battles. God will make you victorious through everything. God will do everything for you that you can't do for yourself. Through God's strength grace mercy love power help support hope. That God has got for you. When people lack compassion sympathy empathy. Trust that your Heavenly Father God Almighty absolutely cherishes you and nurtures you completely. With God you can do everything. God adores you.

There is power through the holy spirit where God dwells within your soul. God will miraculously heal cleanse sanctify Glorify your soul always and forevermore. When you have got the unconditional love of God within your heart and soul. God will bless you with God's love grace mercy hope gratitude. Through God's miraculous healing powers. God will bless you and reward you. With excellent health spiritually emotionally physically mentally. God will make you strong powerful courageous. Through your painful problems. God is there. God will save your soul through it all. God will make it possible for you to conquer your impossible battles. In God's Perfect and Amazing Timing. God's Timing and your Timing will align up together. God will deliver you from your most difficult problems. God will take away your suffering. Through God's powerful love acceptance mercy.

God will give you hope when you are burdened. God will remove your troubles. The only thing in the end that you can always depend upon the most. Is God's Everlasting Eternal faith love hope you have in God. God will heal your broken relationships. God will restore you when you feel hopeless. God will grant you all of your desires of your heart. When people don't relate to you agree with you understand you. Trust that your Glorious Father God Almighty. Knows you better than anyone else does. God will give you strength when you feel helpless. God will give you courage when people are mean to you. God will heal your soul through everything. God will love you always. God will love you when people don't value you. God will bless you when people don't relate to you. God will be there to set you totally free from everything. When you feel low spirited trust that God will make you feel better. God will bless you and reward you. With joy peace happiness positivity hope contentment inspiration. God's truths insights laws revelations. With God there is always positivity hope for a better brighter truthful blessed rewarding future. God will comfort you in times of hurt. God will exalt your spirits in times of sorrow. God will always bless you and love your soul forevermore. God will bring to you the best people. Who have a close relationship with God. Who will become your lifelong friends. God will help you.

God's love grace mercy holiness care God has got for you. Will take away all fear anxiety concern doubt hurt grief insecurity uncertainty within your soul. God loves you beyond your comprehension. God loves you beyond your understanding. God loves you more than you can fathom. God will pick your spirits up when you feel down. God will love you always. God will exalt your spirits through everything. God will always be there for you. When people turn against you. God will save you by setting you free through it all. God will comfort you in times of sadness. God will help you when you feel helpless.

God will always be there to guide lead help support encourage you. When you are feeling down in despair. Trust that your Faithful Righteous Loving Father God is always close to you loving you.

Religious Quotes Book 3

No matter how hopeless you might feel with your impossible battles. Trust that God has got a meaningful and rewarding future ahead of you. God will deliver save break all of your chains rescue set you totally free from your painful battles. God will reveal himself to you. When you open up your heart and soul to God. Through prayer going to church reading God's word. God can do what you can't do. God will make your impossible problems possible for you to conquer. In God's Perfect and Amazing Timing. Make God your world all everything anchor strength hope love positivity saviour deliverer helper healer companion throughout everything in your life.

Only God has got the power courage strength grace mercy love peace. To save you from your impossible battles. God will perform the biggest miraculous supernatural miracles and wonders on you. To heal you from your sicknesses illnesses heartache pain grievances. When people do you wrong. Love and forgive them. Pray a kind good loving prayer for them. The more Christ Like you become through the power of the holy spirit. The more Jesus Christ Almighty will save you from all of your sins. Walk with God through all of your trials and tribulations. God will see you through everything really well.

God absolutely loves you and adores you more than you can imagine. God will bless love reward forgive transform build you up forever and ever. Love people who mistreat you unfairly. Forgive people who reject you. God will exalt your spirits when you are hurting. God will take you right out of any dark place you are in. God will bring you into God's light of God's love help grace mercy peace. God knows all of the cries of your heart. God will show up in your life when you least expect it. God loves you and cares about you more than anything. God will fill your life up with Christ Like friends. Who will be good to you. By keeping you company. Just when you thought that you couldn't make it. God turns up by bringing you the best people places career opportunities possibilities.

When people mistreat you unfairly. Forgive and love them. Then God will forgive and love you. God will step into your life. By turning your whole life around for the better. Through your worst situations you go through. God is there even when you may think that God isn't. Take it by faith. That you have got a faithful God. Who is always there for you. When you are always faithful devoted committed to God.

Then God will always be devoted committed to you. With God you have got absolutely everything you will ever need. Without God you have got nothing. In Heaven everything everyone everywhere will be Perfect Magnificent Harmonious Divine Pure Beautiful.

God will make you Perfect in God's Image. In The Paradise of Heaven for all of Eternity. In Heaven there will be no more pain no more suffering no more depression no more sorrow no more despair no more grief. God is with you when people reject you. God will love you when you are hurting. God will make you happy when you are sad. God will bring you joy through your sorrow. God will comfort you through your heartache. God will sooth you through your grief. God knows so well everything you struggle with and suffer with. God will give you the strength hope courage for you to carry on in this world. God will give you hope when you feel powerless. God will give you the will never to give up. God loves you more than anything.

God will make you strong. When people don't treat you very well. God will love you when you are hurting. God will always bless love reward help heal satisfy delight fulfil you through everything. When people turn against you be good to them. When people reject you forgive them. When people mistreat you unfairly love them. When people wound you very badly. Forgive them and pray a loving kind good prayer for them. God will save you from all of your sins past present future. God has got great plans to prosper heal restore you from everything. In God's Perfect and Majestic Timing. God will make your life a lot more bearable easier manageable for you to cope with.

God will find a way out of your hardest battles addictions trials tribulations. When you feel like there is no way out. God will definitely rescue save deliver find the right way out for you. God will make your life positive great truthful rewarding meaningful thrilling exciting adventurous awe inspiring fabulous always and forevermore. God will make your impossible battles possible for you to conquer. With God all things are possible. When you feel helpless hopeless powerless with your battles addictions sicknesses heartache pain grievances. Trust that God will set you totally free through it all. God absolutely loves and adores all of God's believers who are devoted faithful committed to God. God is always there.

When there is life there will always be hope for all of us. God knows all of the cries of your heart. God will comfort you at all times. When people don't accept you pray for them. Love everyone always. You can't get on with everyone. Not everyone is going to like you and that's okay. Be with people who love value appreciate care about you treasure cherish you. God will bless you with the best people who will become your closest truest favourite friends. You grow learn become stronger better resilient closer powerful to God. When you experience your most challenging battles. God's mercy grace compassion love peace forgiveness. God loves you for sure.

Will heal you from all of your battles in God's Perfect and Amazing Timing. God will save heal deliver set you totally free from your sicknesses diseases brokenness hardships troubles burdens. God knows all of the desires of your heart. God will bring you new Christ

Like friends. Who will become your lifelong friends. When people abandon you trust that God is with you. God will open up amazing doors that you could never of dreamed possible. When people leave you in your life. Trust that God has got a plan for you. God will bring new people into your life. Don't put your trust in man . Always put your complete trust in God. God will never ever leave you.

God will never let you down hurt you disappoint you. When people disappoint you know that God still loves you. God will bring the right people into your life. God will always answer all of your prayers. In God's Perfect and Outstanding Timing.

Religious Quotes Book 4

 od will always grant you all of your needs and desires of your heart and soul forevermore. God loves you. You are God's Precious Child Forever and Ever. On Earth and in The Paradise of Heaven for all of Eternity Forever to Come Forevermore. God loves you beyond your comprehension. God loves you beyond your understanding. God loves you more than you can fathom. When tragedy strikes in your life. Trust that God will show up by helping healing saving rescuing delivering setting you totally free from everything. God has got the power to do anything and everything for you in your life. God is your Healer Restorer Saviour Deliverer Redeemer Life Line Helper Greatest Hope. God is forever and always with you through it all.

You can rely and depend on God all of the time. God will never ever let you down hurt you disappoint you. Everyone has got unfair and difficult battles. That all of us are going through. God will always make everything better for you. God will give you the positivity hope special knowledge love kindness goodness appreciation rich divinity. For you to carry on in this world. When everything feels hopeless in your life. God will show up by giving you positivity and hope.

For you to carry on in this difficult world. God will give you the power. For you to be an overcomer and a conqueror in God. With God there is always positivity and hope for a very bright rewarding meaningful inspirational future. God will make your impossible battles possible for you to conquer. Through God's Amazing Grace Mercy love Compassion Care Generosity Forgiveness Healing Powers Magical Help Divine Intervention. God will do everything you can't do in your life. God will always take good care of you through all of your painful problems. Always live in God's Heavenly Kingdom. Don't live in the world's ways. God will work through you powerfully to heal you completely. God will always make a way through all of your challenging battles. God absolutely loves you and adores you completely. God loves to bless and reward God's Precious Children.

God will make you lucky fortunate blessed privileged always and forevermore. God loves to bless and reward God's Precious Children. Move on from people who are cruel mean nasty unfair to you. Have friends who never mistreat you unfairly. God will always bless you and reward you forevermore. The more compassionate sympathetic empathetic kind loving good fair you become to everyone. The more God will bless you and reward you. Have friends who respect appreciate value adore love nurture cherish you. Don't have friends who hurt you. Karma comes back around for all of us. God is love.

When you are always kind loving good to people. Then people will always be kind loving good to you. But if you mistreat people unfairly. Then people will mistreat you unfairly. God's love will conquer everything. God's love will always win. God's love is the answer to everything. Always build people up who tear you down. Be kind to people who are unfair to you. Love people who do you wrong. Always be positive and empowering to people. Never be negative and disempowering to anyone. God is always there.

You will always reap what you will sow. God will always build you up exalt uplift bless reward help satisfy delight support guide save deliver purify sanctify enlighten empower give you all of the positivity and hope for a wonderful future. God will amaze inspire enlighten enliven bless reward entice excite empower love help support guide exalt encourage you always and forevermore. Always find your identity in The Lord Jesus Christ Almighty. Don't find your identity in people. The Lord Jesus Christ Almighty is your Awesome Saviour. God loves you more than you can ever imagine. God won't ever let you go without anything. God loves to bless and reward God's Precious Children. God will do what you can't do. God will make your impossible battles possible for you to conquer. God will give you hope to live your life. God is always there for you through everything you will ever go through in your life. God loves you a lot.

God will make the most powerful breakthroughs happen for you. Through God's Amazing Grace Love Mercy Compassion Forgiveness Help Support. Your most impossible battles that you are really suffering with. God will make you victorious triumphant powerful through it all. Always be with people who build you up. Don't be with people who tear you down. Always have friends who respect appreciate value love accept you. God's Powerful Unconditional Love God has got for you. Will wipe away your most impossible battles you are struggling with in your life. God will help you to cope better with you challenging problems. God will love you forever and ever.

On Earth and in The Paradise of Heaven for all of Eternity Forever to come Forevermore. God will always save you from all of your sins. God is Everlasting Eternal Pure Righteous Divine Majestic Magnificent Blissful Tranquil Surreal Serene Uplifted Exalted in every Perfect and Amazing Way. Always discover God's Special Knowledge. When you do God will always bless you and reward you abundantly. Always rely on God. Don't rely in man. Always put all of your hope in God. Worship Honour Glorify God first above everyone. When people let you down hurt you disappoint you. God is with you.

Turn to your Faithful Righteous Loving Holy Father God Almighty. God will never disappoint you. God loves you and adores you completely. God's love for you is very Powerful Beautiful Magnificent Divine Holy Righteous Sublime Tranquil Blissful always and forevermore. With God you can do everything you have always dreamed of in your life. God allows you to suffer with impossible battles addictions sorrows sicknesses. So you can reach out to God in prayer to be healed by God. God is always there for you through everything you go through in your life. God loves to bless and reward God's Precious Children. God will reveal to you God's insights truths laws revelations Special Knowledge. God has got a purpose for your existence. When people keep on disappointing you. Take time out for yourself to pray to your Perfect Father God Almighty. God is love.

Find your own inner peace inner joy inner happiness. When people don't understand you love them. When people judge you forgive them. When people hurt you be good to them. When you help yourself a lot by ceasing your unhealthy habits. God will bless you and reward you with positivity joy love excitement happiness. God will give you all of the help support guidance motivation determination resilience discipline strength courage power. For you to be victorious triumphant powerful through all of your impossible battles. God will intervene in your life by solving your battles for you.

When you have battles addictions sorrows sicknesses. Trust that God will give you the courage strength power hope positivity. God will give you the victory to get through it all. God has overcome the world by sending Jesus to die on the cross to save you from your sins. God will always set you totally free from everything. God will provide for you the right people. Who will have a close relationship with God. Who will become your lifelong friends. Your impossible battles are your way to God. What you suffer with. God will never forsake you.

Will better grow you closer deeper stronger real powerful to God. You learn your most valuable important greatest lessons. From going through your biggest painful problems. God will always fix you. God will make a way out of your challenging impossible battles. God will remove from you all of your impossible battles. Your painful problems that you are suffering with a lot. That you feel that are out of your control. God will make a way out. God will reveal to you everything you need to know do see hear. Through the power of the holy spirit from God. Life can be hard. Relationships can be hard. Always love and forgive everyone who hurts you unfairly. God will always set you totally free from everything. You are your own person. You make all of your own choices and decisions. You know what is best for you better than anyone. When you have got faith love hope in God. Nothing and no one can ever hurt you. God will make you victorious triumphant powerful through everything.

Always love and forgive people who mistreat you unfairly. Then God will love and forgive you. God can do anything and everything that is beyond your control. God has got the power to remove your impossible battles. God's Presence is very Powerful in Your life. God will do what you can't do. God won't let you go without anything. God loves to bless and reward God's Precious Children Abundantly. God will awaken renew enlighten empower sanctify rectify bless love reward give you hope positivity kindness goodness compassion through everything you will ever go through in your life.

What is impossible to you is possible to God. No matter what you are suffering with. Trust that God will find a way out for you. Accept let go surrender your difficult battles you suffer with. Doing this will help you to cope better with a lot less stress. God is going to make you victorious triumphant powerful. God will deliver you from everything you no longer want in your life. God's Perfect Love will Cast Out All Fear Anxiety Doubt Uncertainty Insecurity Bad Health. One reason why you suffer with your impossible battles. Is so that you can fight for your faith love hope in God. God will always help and support you. God is guiding you on your destiny of your life.

Your impossible battles are there to teach you about God's truths and laws. What you suffer with will draw you closer to God. If we didn't have impossible battles to get through there would be no point to our existence. And no point to our faith love hope in God. God will reveal to you all of God's truths insights laws revelations. Your battles teach you about God's Special Knowledge. God will surround you with beautiful people. Who will appreciate like value enjoy love cherish treasure you completely. God will renew replenish build exalt transform redeem heal restore save rescue give your life truth meaning insights revelations. God will give you the spiritual nourishment to your heart and soul. That you need to survive living your life on this Earth. God loves you more than you can imagine.

God will heal mend fix restore help support bless reward bring you peace joy happiness positivity goodness love excitement kindness compassion sympathy empathy forgiveness. Through all of your trials burdens tribulations troubles. Your challenging battles are there to guide you to God. Nothing comes easily in this world. Everything you will ever do will require your positive effort persistence perseverance patience time creativity concentration attention. God will bring the right people into your life. Who will help support guide value adore appreciate love accept like you. God will enrich love guide help you.

God will bless enlighten enliven reward help support guide you. When you are going through your worst low valley's in your life. If you never ever give up you will win all of your battles. In God's Perfect and Amazing Timing. God will conquer all of your battles. When people try to get to you in unfair ways. Love and forgive them. When people try to annoy you. Be kind and good to them. You grow stronger develop advance deeper richer more powerful in God. Through your most challenging battles. God can do anything and everything. God will give you the positivity hope strength power. For you to be Prosperous Courageous Fun Loving Joyful Peaceful Happy.

Your most difficult battles will help you to grow learn develop understand your faith love hope in God a lot better. God will make you triumphant through everything. No matter how much you are suffering with your impossible battles. God will intervene by saving you. Trust that God will give you the victory. You learn your biggest lessons. From your greatest pain and suffering. God will turn your challenges into abundant blessings and rewards. Your impossible battles you suffer with. Are possible for God to conquer. God will make you surmountable for you to be victorious triumphant powerful through everything. God will make your life a lot better worthwhile healed restored replenished renewed truthful meaningful purposeful prosperous. God will always be there for you.

God's love is unconditional endless everlasting pure innocent divine clean righteous tranquil blissful surreal serene beautiful magnificent lovely great amazing. God will make you victorious from your biggest battles that you are fighting to conquer. No battle is too hard for God to conquer. We are all unique. Everyone has got a different cross to bear. Everyone has got different weaknesses they are battling with. And everyone has got their own strengths as well. God will give you the inspiration motivation resilience discipline special knowledge. That God wants to reveal to you. God will do what you can't do.

With God everything is possible to accomplish. God will help you to win your battles. God loves to bless and reward God's Precious Children. God won't ever leave you. God will work Miraculously on you by Performing Almighty Amazing Incredible Out of This World Meaningful Rewarding Truthful Helpful Wonderful Prosperous Blessings Rewards Delights Surprises on you. God will comfort you in times of distress. God will make you happy when you are sad. God will love you when you are hurting. Imitation is the highest form of flattery. God has gifted each of us uniquely. With God's Special Knowledge. God loves you more than you can ever imagine.

Jesus Christ Almighty is going to return to this world very soon. To heal the whole world by making Heaven on Earth. God created you in your mother's womb. God knows you better than anyone else knows you. God knows you better than you know yourself. God is a Loving Gracious Merciful Forgiving Magnificent Faithful Pure Righteous God. God will bring you new friends. When you join activities like tafe university work church. God always thinks of you. God will give you the giftings of awareness compassion sympathy empathy understanding endless divine pure clean holy righteous love kindness goodness fairness. Praying to God reading the bible being in the state of grace with the power of the holy spirit going to church. Are the most powerful things that you will ever do. God is always with you.

God will make you triumphant through your most difficult battles. Your battles teach you about God's truths and laws. God will bless you and reward you big time. When you conquer your addictions despairs sorrows sicknesses heartache pain grief. When you feel helpless with conquering your impossible battles. Trust that God will make a way when there seems to be no way. God blesses and rewards those people who help themselves. God will bless you and reward you doubly. When you help other people. God is there.

God will bless you and reward you with. God's true rich divinity truths insights laws revelations prosperous meaningful knowledge. God will save you from all of your sins. God loves you more than you can imagine. God won't let you go without anything. You will overcome your impossible battles. When you are ready. In God's Perfect and Amazing Timing. Nothing is impossible to God. God will give you everything you are looking for in your life. Always work on your mental physical spiritual emotional health. God will always bless you and reward you abundantly. God will give you plans purpose.

God teaches you the most about God yourself people. With what you suffer with and struggle with the most. Don't ever rebel against yourself. When people patronize you bless them. When people are unfair to you be kind to them. When people belittle you be good to them. You will always reap what you will sow. Everything you give out will come back to you. If you feel good and uplifted inside yourself then you will make other people feel good and uplifted. If you feel bad and unhappy within yourself then you will make other people feel bad and unhappy. God will take your spirit to The Paradise of Heaven. In God's Perfect and Amazing Timing. God will make your spirit Perfect in God's Image. In The Paradise of Heaven there will be no more pain no more suffering no more depression no more heartache no more sadness no more sickness no more disease no more grief forever to come forevermore. God loves you always.

Death is the Beginning of New Exciting Eternal Everlasting Life in The Kingdom of Heaven. With our Father God Almighty and our Loved Ones For All of Eternity Forevermore. Always work hard at increasing your peaceful joyful positive happy go lucky emotions. Always forgive and love people who hurt you. Then God will forgive and love you. God loves to always bless and reward God's Precious Children. Be your own person. Don't follow the crowd. Be an individual with your own ideas. Always find your own identity in The Lord Jesus Christ.

Always put God first above everyone and everything in this world. Jesus Christ Almighty has overcome the world by dying on the cross. Always be faithful devoted committed to God. Then God will always be faithful devoted committed to you. Be quick to forgive people for their shortcomings. Never hold any grudges towards anyone who mistreats you unfairly. Always and forever love everyone. Gods love is out of this world incredibly enticing brilliantly amazing unconditionally loving beautifully magnificent. God will never give up on you if your never give up on God. God is always with you in it all.

Never have any cares in the world. God will conquer all of your impossible battles for you. God will always make you a conqueror and an overcomer through everything. You can never control what is going on around you. You can only control how you choose to respond. Don't react to people's cruelty ever. God will always make you Almighty Courageous Bold Daring Fearless Unafraid Healthy Compassionate Sympathetic Empathetic Forgiving Unconditionally Loving Kind Good Fair Just Always and Forevermore. God will heal all of your wounds from your past. God is your Restorer Redeemer Deliverer Rescuer Life Line Helper Healer Always and Forever and Ever. God can do everything and anything in your life. God has got all of the power to save rescue help heal deliver restore replenish rectify sanctify redeem set you totally free from everything in your life. With God all things will always be possible for you to conquer.

Your true real favourite faithful devoted committed friends. Who love and accept you for who you are. Will never leave you nor forsake you. God will give you the strength courage power for you to be victorious triumphant powerful through everything in your life. God will give you a clean bill of health always and forevermore. God will give you a giant leap of faith with you overcoming all of your impossible battles. God loves to pour out God's Blessings Rewards Surprises Delights to all of God's Children. God will always get you through all of your painful problems always and forevermore.

God will take away your battles you are fighting to overcome. In God's Superb and Awesome Timing. God will set you totally free from everything. God will give you the courage power strength for you to overcome by being victorious triumphant powerful through everything. God will make you courageous. God will conquer your impossible battles for you. In God's Perfect and Amazing Timing. Hallelujah Praise The Lord Jesus Christ Almighty. Everyone has been defeated and overcome by some impossible battle. That has taken over their life. God will step in by saving you totally. God is with you.

God will heal your wounded heart. God will take away your pain suffering anxiety heartache grief. God will save you through it all. Some people can always see the positivity love goodness beauty compassion sympathy empathy in you. Other people are blinded to seeing your positive and good side. Some people will always be your faithful devoted committed friends. Other people can betray your friendship. There will always be new friends that you will be able to make. God won't ever forsake you or abandon you nor leave you. God will always be with you through everything you will ever endure in your life. The more powerful your faith love hope in God is. The more God will perform God's miraculous and supernatural healing powers on you. God will deliver you from everything in your life. God will bring new supportive understanding encouraging kind hearted good willed friends into your life. Who are close and faithful to God.

When people are against you love them. When people don't value you forgive them. When people reject you pray for them. Your battles give your faith love hope in God strength hope positivity courage. To cope better with your difficult problems. God will end your painful battles completely. God will mend fix heal your broken heart. God can do everything and anything. Make the most of every moment of every day. Nobody knows when their time will be up. Live every day to the fullest. Don't take offense when people don't agree with what you say. Not everyone will accept you for who you are. And that's okay. God will always see you through all of your trials.

Your impossible battles that you suffer with. God will Glorify Restore Sanctify Rectify Save Deliver you from Miraculously. God will give you a better life better health better opportunities and possibilities. God will give you better ways of coping in more useful and beneficial ways of dealing with everything in your life. God will make you triumphant through all of your challenging problems. God's unconditional love will save you from all of your hardest battles sicknesses diseases illnesses poverty depression sadness despairs sorrows grievances always and forevermore. God has got the power to set you totally free from all of your impossible battles. God is love.

God has got all of the Powerful Omniscient Amazing Grace Endless Mercy Supernatural Victorious Courage. To Save you from Everything. When you feel powerless helpless hopeless in your painful battles. Trust that God will step in by making you an overcomer and an conqueror. God doesn't judge you with your outward appearance. God judges you according to the intentions of your heart. Don't judge anyone. God teaches you the most about God yourself other people and your life experiences. Through your most painful battles. God loves to bless and reward God's Precious Children abundantly. You can't get on well with everyone. Some people will bring out the best in you. Other people will bring out the worst in you. God will always bless you and reward you big time.

In The Paradise of Heaven there will be no more pain no more suffering no more depression no more heartache no more sorrow no more despair no more sickness. God will take your spirit to The Paradise of Heaven in God's Perfect and Amazing Timing. God will make your spirit Perfect in God's Image in The Kingdom of Heaven for all of Eternity. Your impossible battles you suffer with. That have overtaken your will. That you feel like you can't escape from. God is always there to deliver you from completely. With God everything will always be possible to achieve overcome conquer surpass accomplish. God will always make your life better and well improved.

If you never ever give up on God then God will never ever give up on you. Always live your life in God's Unconditional Endless Love Kindness Goodness Excitement Peace Joy Happiness. Don't live your life in fear. God is always with you through everything you will ever go through good and bad. God will take away your pain suffering anxiety heartache grief. In God's Perfect and Amazing Timing. God absolutely loves you and adores you. In God's Perfect and Outstanding Timing. God will help you to cope a lot better in your life.

In positive kind loving good peaceful joyful happy fair ways. Always be with people who accept appreciate value love cherish understand you. Don't be with people who don't love and accept you. Not everyone is going to like and accept you for who you are. Stay close to those people who are special valuable precious important to you. When people don't agree with what you are saying to them. Understand that all of us have got a different cross to bear. Sometimes all of us can inflict our own negativity judgements criticisms cruelty onto each other in our lives. Accept and surrender to God. Your difficult battles. Then God will make it easier manageable bearable for you. God will help you to see you through everything in your life. God will always give you everything you are looking for in your life. God will give you all of your needs desires wishes wants yearnings longings of your heart always and forever.

Your impossible battles make you strong courageous powerful with your faith love hope in God. God will make you victorious triumphant powerful through it all. You are an adult now. You make all of your own choices and decisions. Don't let your parents tell you what to do by controlling you. Keep on being kind loving good generous helpful supportive compassionate encouraging forgiving fair just to everyone. Don't put up with people's mistreatment of you. Distance yourself from people who bully you badly. Be will people who treat you right and well. In positive kind loving good caring gentle fair just ways always and forevermore. God will get you out of everything bad.

God has overcome the world by sending Jesus Christ Almighty to die on the cross to save you from your sins. When Jesus Christ Almighty was living in the world. Jesus Christ Almighty said that everyone will have sorrow in this world. God will show up at the right time. When you thought it was all over. Never give up hope. God will make your life a lot better. Hold on God will heal save rescue deliver unleash all of your chains set you totally free. From your painful battles completely. Always be with positive and empowering people.

Don't be with negative and disempowering people. You will be happy that way. When people mistreat you unfairly forgive and love them. Then God will forgive and love you. Don't harm your own health with unhealthy addictions. When people are cruel mean nasty unfair to you. Be kind loving good to yourself. You learn develop advance grow mature. From going through your biggest pain and suffering. Throughout your whole life. You learn your most important valuable greatest lessons. By going through your worst painful battles. Don't let people who don't have your best interests within their hearts. To influence you by making your decisions. Always make your own decisions. Let God make all of your decisions for you. Don't let people make your decisions for you. You don't have to do anything you don't want to do. God will turn everything into your own favour.

Don't let other people to affect you in the slightest. With their negativity cruelty judgements criticisms belittlement of you. When your health is failing you. Trust that God will intervene by healing you saving you rescuing you delivering you helping you setting you totally free from all of your sicknesses illnesses diseases heartache pain grievances throughout your whole life. Always stay positive kind loving good fair just uplifted exalted prosperous blessed rewarded in high spirits. Through your darkest moments. God will give you all of the answers in your life. To help you to achieve by getting ahead with all of your aspirations. God will help love guide forgive save you.

God will empower enlighten build you up exalt uplift bring you peace joy happiness prosperity compassion kindness goodness love fairness throughout your whole life. God loves you more than you can ever imagine. God will do what you can't do. God won't let you go without anything ever. God will always heal restore sustain deliver save help support you. God will always get you through everything you will ever go through in your life. God will give you a peaceful joyful happy death. Where you will die in the state of Grace and go straight to The Paradise of Heaven for all of Eternity. God is love.

Where you will be with God and your past dearly loved ones in Heaven forever and ever. Don't be with people who devalue degrade mock ridicule you. Be with people who respect appreciate value nurture accept you for who you are. Some people will always mistreat you unfairly. Then other people will always love accept value appreciate adore respect you. Not everyone will have your best interests within their hearts. Don't give your information to people you can't trust. God will always bless you and reward you big time. When you are always with the right and best people. God won't ever bless you and reward you. When you are with the wrong people. You learn your most major life lessons from God. Through experiencing your painful problems. God will always rescue you from everything.

Learn how to stand up for yourself in kind assertive gentle firm ways. When people treat you in sarcastic patronizing condescending ways. God's love conquers everything. God's love will always win. God's love is the answer to everything. Don't be with people who bully you. With their sarcasm cruelty negativity judgements towards you. Always be with people who treat you right and well. With respect dignity grace forevermore. Always make friends who treat you with positivity respect dignity grace appreciation love gratefulness thankfulness kindness goodness fairness justness forevermore.

Always be with people who love adore accept appreciate nurture value cherish you. Not everyone will like you and that's okay. Always be with people who bring out the best in you. Who uplift you who build you up. Don't be with people who tear you down. God will get everything right for you in your life. God will give you the best life ever. That you have possibly ever dreamed to have. God wants the best for you. God loves you and adores you completely. With your faith love hope in God you will be able to get through everything that you are struggling with and suffering with in your life. God won't ever abandon you nor forsake you or leave you. God will heal you.

God will bless you and reward you with a meaningful wise fulfilling sustaining worthwhile satisfying fruitful rewarding wholesome life. God will do what you can't do. God won't let you go without anything ever. God will save you and set you totally free from everything in your life. God will give you everything you are looking for in your life. God will save you from all of your sins. God will heal deliver mend fix restore sustain rectify sanctify you from all of your sicknesses illnesses diseases heartache pain grievances always and forevermore. God will give you the power strength courage to be an conqueror through all of your battles. Nothing is impossible to God. God will make you triumphant through all of your impossible battles. God will give you everything you are looking for in your life always. God's love will conquer all of your difficulties sicknesses addictions.

God will do the impossible for you in your life. God will perform the most amazing miracles and wonders on you. God will heal restore fix mend replenish your health finances relationships always and forevermore. God knows you better than anyone else knows you. God knows you better than you know yourself. God has got a blessed rewarding joyful peaceful happy go lucky meaningful helpful supportive empowering enlightening positive future ahead of you.

God loves you beyond your comprehension. God loves you beyond your understanding. God loves you more than you can fathom.

If you never give up you will always win all of your battles. God will answer all of your prayers. In God's Perfect and Amazing Timing. Always forgive and love people who mistreat you unfairly. Then God will always forgive and love you. Sometimes your own parents sisters brothers can cause you heartache pain grief. But don't worry God has overcome the world. By sending Jesus Christ Almighty to die on the cross by saving you from your sins. When people say cruel nasty mean unfair words to you. Always say positive kind good loving fair just words to them. God will always keep you safe well protected.

In The Paradise of Heaven everything everyone everywhere will be Perfect Prestigious Magnificent Divine Blissful Tranquil Surreal Serene Joyful Peaceful Happy Glorious Righteous Pure Holy Supreme Significant Always and Forevermore. Don't listen to the put downs cruelty mockery sarcasm belittlement negativity of other people. Always find your own identity in The Lord Jesus Christ Almighty. Don't find your identity in people. God will always set you free from all of your iniquities sicknesses addictions illnesses diseases heartache pain grievances forevermore. God will heal restore replenish build you up exalt perfect all of your ways help guide support love forgive you through everything in your life always. God always knows what is best for you. God has always got your best interests within God's heart forevermore. God will always help you.

When you are feeling helpless in your impossible battles. Trust that God will deliver save rescue set you totally free from everything. God will comfort you in times of distress. God will make you happy when you are sad. God will love you when you are hurting. God will give you that giant leap of faith that you are looking for. For God to help heal save rescue deliver support you. Through all of your sorrows despairs troubles burdens sicknesses illnesses diseases hurts upsets always and forevermore. God will make all of your dreams come true especially for you. God absolutely loves you and adores you completely. From the beginning and until the end of your time on this Earth. God will always get you through everything in your life.

God will make possible for you to conquer your impossible battles. In God's Perfect and Amazing Timing. Nothing is impossible to God. Sometimes God allows us to suffer with impossible battles. For our character to grow stronger closer deeper powerful richer in God. God will wipe away your fears anxieties addictions sicknesses illnesses diseases heartache pain grievances always and forevermore. God has got the miraculous supernatural healing powers. To heal save rescue deliver you from. Your sicknesses illnesses diseases addictions heartache pain grievances always and forevermore. God won't ever forsake you nor abandon you leave you.

Pray for your enemies. God will turn everything around for the better. In God's Perfect and Amazing Timing. God will fix everything for you always. God will look after your health for you. God will transform mend restore fix replenish your bad health miraculously.

God loves you more than you can ever imagine. God will do what you can't do. Nothing is impossible to God. God loves you and adores you forever and ever. God's love is out of this world brilliant incredible hopeful promising positive powerful faithful devoted committed Eternal Everlasting Always and Forevermore. With God everything will always be possible to accomplish. But without God everything will be impossible to accomplish. God can do all things forevermore.

God will make your spirit Perfect in God's Image in Heaven. In Heaven everything everyone everywhere will be Perfect Blissful Tranquil Surreal Serene Joyful Peaceful Happy Ecstatic Harmonious Magnificent Majestic Prestigious Fantastic Marvellous Awesome Always and For all of Eternity with God Forever to Come Forevermore. Always find your identity in The Lord Jesus Christ Almighty. Don't find your identity in people. Jesus Christ Almighty died on the cross to save you from your sins. By giving you the Gift of Eternal Life in The Paradise of Heaven with God for all of Eternity.

God loves you beyond your comprehension. God loves you beyond your understanding. God loves you more than you can fathom. God will give you everything you are looking for in your life. God will conquer your impossible battles for you. In God's Perfect and Majestic Timing. Nothing is impossible to God. God will always be there for you. In times of sorrow loneliness heartache despair sadness pain grief always and forevermore. If you always focus on God. Then God will always focus on you. God will help support you.

God knows and understands your pain and suffering you go through. God has got an Almighty plan to make everything better for you. Love people who hurt you. Be kind to people who are unfair to you. Respect people who reject you. Be good to people who are cruel to you. Karma comes around for all of us. When you are always positive loving kind good fair just to everyone. Then that's the way how other people will treat you in return. When you always do the right thing by never hurting people emotionally. Then God will bless you and reward you. With a wonderful amazing incredible out of this world blessed rewarding meaningful splendid spectacular beautiful life for yourself. You treat people how you would like to be treated in return. Never mistreat anyone unfairly. Always do kind loving good deeds to everyone you know and everyone you meet. God will always help inspire encourage support motivate you in your life. God will always be there for you to love bless reward fulfill sustain you.

One day all of us are going to meet God on Judgment Day. God will ask you how did you help other people. God will ask you did you love people. God will bless you and reward you big time in your life. God will keep you in strong health. By preserving your health. Through the power of the holy spirit from God that dwells within you. God will answer all of your prayers. In God's Perfect and Amazing Timing. God will save you from your sadness sicknesses sorrows addictions despairs always and forevermore. Always be respectful considerate positive kind loving good fair just to everyone. Never mistreat anyone unfairly. God will cleanse restore control your emotions.

God will place God's anointing upon you. God will heal deliver save you from your sicknesses illnesses diseases heartache pain grief. God will heal bless save rescue deliver help support guide exalt uplift better your health to excellent health always and forevermore. Always have positivity hope hold on. God's blessings rewards breakthroughs delights surprises are just around the corner. There is no problem too big or small that God can't conquer. When there is a will. God will always find a way out. Just when you thought you couldn't make it. God will show up. God will conquer your impossible battles one day. That you have been struggling with and suffering with for decades and decades. God will find a way out of it all.

With God's help everything will be possible to accomplish. God will intercede in your life. God will deliver save rescue set you totally free from everything. In God's Perfect and Amazing Timing. God loves to bless and reward God's Precious Children. God will perform the biggest miraculous miracles and wonders and breakthroughs on you. God will step in and conquer what you are finding impossible to let go of. God will take away all of your troubles tribulations burdens trials. God will restore what you have lost. God will bless you and reward you big time in your life. God has got the power to intervene in your life. God can do everything and anything. God is there for you.

God knows so well everything that you struggle with and suffer with. Shall God make all of your burdens light for you to carry. God will intervene in your life. God will take away your addictions despairs sorrows sicknesses illnesses diseases grievances. God will give you God's Special knowledge peace of mind joy happiness positivity hope prosperous excitement restoration. God will do what you can't do. God's love conquers everything. God's love will always win. God's love is the answer to everything. In The Paradise of Heaven there will be no more pain no more suffering no more sickness no more heartache no more depression no more grief. God is close to you.

Everything everyone everywhere in The Kingdom of Heaven will be completely Ecstatic Jolly Positive Harmonious Peaceful Happy Go Lucky Blissful Tranquil Surreal Serene Perfect Holy Righteous Pure Clean Magnificent Majestic Prestigious Divine Always and Forever To Come Forevermore For All of Eternity. Hallelujah Praise The Lord Jesus Christ Almighty Amen. God will make your Spirit Perfect in God's Image in The Kingdom of Heaven For All Of Eternity. God will fix mend save rescue deliver unleash all of your chains redeem replenish renew sanctify rectify restore help support you always.

God knows exactly everything you are suffering with. God is teaching you what you need to learn. From your impossible battles. God won't ever abandon you forsake you or leave you. God will make you strong courageous bold daring sublime calm at peace joyful happy well rested always and forevermore. God has got a place for you in The Paradise of Heaven with God and your past dearly loved ones forever to come forevermore for all of Eternity. God will make you victorious triumphant powerful sustained restored replenished joyful peaceful happy go lucky fortunate blessed privileged. When you die in the

State of God's Grace and when you believe in God and The Paradise of Heaven. God will take you to Heaven one day. Always do the right thing by being respectful considerate positive compassionate sympathetic empathetic. God will bless you big time.

Don't ever mistreat anyone unfairly. Always be positive kind loving good uplifted fair just respectable considerate to everyone. Always be with people who like accept value adore nurture cherish care about you appreciate you. Don't be with people who don't accept you. God is your rock redeemer saviour refuge restorer life line deliverer helper healer greatest hope. God can do everything you can't do. God will restore what you have lost in your life. God loves you more than you can ever imagine. God will give you everything you are looking for in your life. God won't let you go without anything ever. God will bless and reward your health back to fine and excellent health completely. Open up your heart to God always.

There is power with your faith love hope in God. Knowing The Lord Jesus Christ Almighty will bless sustain reward restore sanctify rectify fix mend save deliver help support set you totally free from all of your troubles trials burdens tribulations. God will do the impossible for you in your life. God will give you positivity and hope in your hopeless circumstances. God will save you through it all. God will bless you and reward you. With God's Special Knowledge Grace Love Mercy Compassion Sympathy Empathy Forgiveness Certainty Goodness. If you never give up on God. God will never give up on you.

Your time will come when you will conquer your long lived battles addictions despairs sicknesses illnesses diseases. God absolutely loves you and adores you. God loves to bless and reward God's Precious Children. Don't ever place any judgment criticism belittlement don't ever condemn anyone with what they suffer with. Always be with people who are positive and empowering. Don't be with people who are negative and disempowering. God won't ever let you go. God will always be there for you when you need God. God will heal save rescue deliver unleash all of your chains set you totally free from everything. Never let anyone stop you believing in God. Be strong courageous bold daring positive with your faith love hope in God. God will always love bless reward be kind good faithful to you.

Don't follow the crowd. Be your own person. With your own ideas identity attitudes characteristics qualities attributes. God has got the healing powers to perform the most miraculous supernatural miracles wonders blessings rewards delights surprises on you. Through God's power of the holy spirit that dwells within you. Be with people who respect consider appreciate value love accept adore cherish you treasure you. Don't be with people who don't accept you. God will do what you can't do. God will heal you from your battles addictions burdens trials troubles tribulations. God loves you.

God loves to bless and reward God's Precious Children. God will do the impossible for you. God will conquer all of your impossible battles for you. God can do anything and everything that is impossible for us human beings to achieve. There is healing powers knowing God.

God will move the biggest mountains for you. God will make you a conqueror and an overcomer in The Lord Jesus Christ Almighty. When you are feeling down in the dumps. Turn to God in prayer. God will uplift elate exalt comfort make you feel a lot better.

God loves you more than you can ever imagine. God wants to bless you and reward you immensely. God's love conquers everything. There is no problem too big or too small that God can't overcome and conquer. God will do the impossible for you in your life always and forevermore. When people reject you accept it. When people no longer want to be your friends. Trust God will bring you new and better friends. There is a light at the end of every tunnel. Every grey cloud has got a silver lining. When there is a will there will always be a way. God will transform you into a wonderfully amazing incredible new creation. Through the Almighty Power of God's Grace and Mercy. God will renew replenish create sustain fulfill bless reward help support you with a healthy mind spirit body soul. Don't take it to heart when people reject you. There are lots and lots of people to meet in the world. God will be by your side forever and ever.

God will give you the positivity hope knowledge motivation determination persistence resilience drive enthusiasm through everything you go through always and forevermore. God will renew replenish exalt heal help support encourage motivate guide direct inspire sanctify rectify you from everything. Through God's Amazing Grace Love Mercy Compassion Forgiveness Certainty Reassurance Comfort Peace Happiness. God will Always and Forever

Restore You From Everything. God knows you better than anyone else knows you. God knows you better than you know yourself. God loves you a lot.

God will heal you from all of your wounds from your past present future always and forevermore. Don't open up your spirit to people who you sense you can't trust. Not everyone will have your best interests within their hearts. Move on from people who mistreat you unfairly. God will guide you to much better people who you will meet. Who will accept love adore value appreciate cherish treasure you just away you are. God is with you when no one else is.

When you feel all alone. Trust that God will bring into your life. The best people who will have a powerful relationship with God. Don't ever judge criticize condemn focus on people's faults flaws mistakes. Love and accept people just the way they are. When nobody else is there for you. God is forever and always so powerfully by your side. Helping loving supporting caring guiding inspiring you in every great and amazing way. Don't give yourself away to people who aren't deserving of you. Give yourself to people who you can trust. Who are worthy and deserving of you. God will guide you to positive loving kind good fair just lovely beautiful great amazing people. Who will become your lifelong friends. Spread your wings put yourself out there. Meet people by making new friends. With the right and best people. God will give you God's Almighty Power Positive Courage Amazing Grace Loving Mercy Compassionate Sympathy through it all.

God will make you victorious triumphant powerful through all of your trials burdens tribulations troubles. God is always on your side through it all. In The Paradise of Heaven there will be no more pain no more suffering no more depression no more sorrow no more sickness no more addictions no more grief. In The Kingdom of Heaven everything everyone everywhere will be Perfect Blissful Tranquil Surreal Serene Joyful Peaceful Happy Ecstatic Always and Forevermore. God will make your Spirit Perfect in God's Image in Heaven For All Of Eternity Forever to Come Forevermore. Gods love

The end of the world is coming. The Lord Jesus Christ Almighty is going to return to this world. To save us all from the corona virus. Jesus Christ Almighty died on the cross to save you from your sins. By giving you the gift of Eternal Life in The Kingdom of Heaven with God. God will never ever fail you. People will fail you by disappointing you. God is completely Perfect but us human beings are imperfect. You learn grow become better evolved advanced more knowledgeable in God. Through going through your most painful problems. You learn your most valuable important greatest lessons. By experiencing your greatest trials and sorrows. God is love.

Imitation is the highest form of flattery. God's Promises Special Knowledge Truths Insights Laws Revelations will Bless You and Reward You Big Time In Your life Always and Forevermore. God is always with you through everything you will ever go through in your life. From the beginning of your time and until the end of your time of this Earth. God and your past dearly loved ones will be with you in The Paradise of Heaven for all of Eternity forever to come forevermore. If you believe in God and The Kingdom of Heaven and dying in The State of Grace. God will take your Spirit to The Kingdom of Heaven one day. For you to join God and your past dearly loved ones in Heaven for all of Eternity forever to come forevermore. God will always love you cherish you treasure you adore you comfort you.

God will help you a lot to cope really well mentally physically spiritually emotionally. God will heal you from everything in your life. Always focus on God and God will always focus on you. The Holy Spirit from God that dwells within your heart and soul. Will heal you from everything that is troubling you. With God you have got everything but without God you have got nothing. Your faith in God will bring you salvation in The Lord Jesus Christ Almighty. Hallelujah Praise The Lord Jesus Christ Almighty Amen. God will answer all of your prayers. In God's Perfect and Amazing Timing. God is there.

Don't listen to the negativity judgements cruelty criticisms nastiness of people. Always be with people who like accept value appreciate adore you for the person you are. Don't turn to people who are angry who belittle degrade patronize you who try to bring you down. Always turn to people who treat you well. God is with you when you feel all alone. God will fulfill sustain help restore fix mend save rescue deliver replenish build you up always and forevermore. Life happens when you are busy making other plans.

God will always be Good Gracious Merciful Grateful Thankful Appreciative. To God's Believers. The Holy Spirit from God that dwells within your Spirit.

Will heal restore fix mend save rescue deliver set you totally free from everything. God will reveal to you through the Power of the Holy Spirit from God. Everything you need to know do see hear believe. Don't have any contact with people who don't have the ability to validate appreciate value accept like approve understand you. When you feel lonely reach out to God and people. God will comfort satisfy reassure you make you feel better love help support you. God will bless you and reward you with joy peace prosperity happiness excitement positivity goodness. Through you trials burdens tribulations troubles. Put all of your faith trust hope love in God. Don't put you trust in man. God will never disappoint you. God loves you Eternally Forever and Ever. God is forever and always there.

Stay well always by protecting yourself from bullies who treat you badly. Always be with people who are positive kind loving good fair just to you. Sometimes when people hurt you badly. It is better to move on from them. By meeting new and better people who don't hurt you. God will give you God's Influential Healing Powers through the holy spirit that is within your spirit from God. The more open in tune aware in touch you become of God's Presence in your life. Always have friends who appreciate nurture value accept like adore enjoy you. Don't have friends you don't value and enjoy you.

God will answer all of your prayers. In God's Perfect and Amazing Timing. God will put your soul at rest. God absolutely loves you and adores you completely. Always forgive and love people who mistreat you unfairly. Then God will always forgive and love you. God will comfort you in times of distress. God will make you happy when you are sad. God will love you when you are hurting. God will always make you fearless and unafraid through everything you go through in your life. God is your Anchor Deliverer Redeemer Saviour Life Line Greatest Hope. When you do kind loving good deeds for people.

God will bless you and reward you with positivity freedom liberation independence. God will help support guide exalt uplift open up your soul totally to The Lord Jesus Christ Almighties truths insights laws revelations Special Knowledge always and forevermore. God is love. God will guide you in all of God's righteous pure innocent blessed rewarding meaningful truthful majestic magnificent divine tranquil peaceful joyful happy go lucky ways. The most important reason why we have been given the gift of life. Is to have a relationship with God. God will make your impossible battles possible for you to conquer. Even through your trials and tribulations. God always goes with you through everything you experience in your life. God can do everything and anything. Trust that God will make a way when there seems to be no way. Through your impossible battles. God will bless you and reward you big time in your life. When you Glorify God.

Knock and the door will be opened. Seek and you shall find. Ask and you shall receive. All of us will always reap what we will sow. God loves to bless and reward God's Precious Children Abundantly. God and God's Angels will always go before us through everything we experience always and forevermore. God is always with you through the good and the bad you go through. God is going to give you the power self control effort energy positivity hope courage strength. For you to be victorious triumphant powerful through everything you will ever endure. What is impossible for you to conquer is possible for God to conquer. God will do what you can't do. God is hope.

God will do the impossible for you in your life. God will set you totally free from your impossible battles. With God everything will be possible for you to conquer. God has got the power to deliver you from the struggle and fight you are going through internally with your battles. God is always there for you through everything you go through in your life. God will always and forever love you. Always be with people who let you be the person you are meant to be. Don't be with people who try to downgrade you. God will make you blessed lucky fortunate privileged. Through everything you will ever go through in your life. God is always and forever with you. God is love.

Always be with people who validate appreciate value accept like approve understand adore you for the person you are. When there is a will there will always be a way. There is a light at the end of every tunnel. Every grey cloud has got a silver lining. The more powerful your faith love hope in God becomes. The stronger deeper resilient disciplined peaceful joyful happy you will become in your life. God is with you through your loneliness heartache pain sadness despairs sorrows grievances. God will always be there to love you nurture you help you support you encourage you adore you value you cherish you treasure you forgive you guide you sustain you motivate you comfort you. God has got the power to bless you for the better.

Always find your identity in The Lord Jesus Christ Almighty. Don't find your identity in people. The Lord Jesus Christ Almighty will always and forever set your spirit totally free from everything. God will always keep you safe and well protected. God loves you beyond your comprehension. God is always there for you through everything you will ever go through in your life. Always be the person God made you to be. All of us are individuals. You make all of your own decisions. You are God's Precious Child. You belong to God. Always be with people who validate appreciate value accept like approve understand adore you for the person you are. God is always for you.

Don't be with people who don't have the ability to validate appreciate nurture value accept like approve of you. God will reveal to you all of God's Special Knowledge Insights Truths Laws Revelations. God will build you up through everything. Always build people up don't tear people down. Your faith love hope in God will see you through everything you will ever go through in your life. When you always focus on God then God will always focus on you. God will give you positivity and hope in your hopeless situations. God will give you all of the victory through your impossible battles. God has got the power to intervene in your life. God is forever with you.

By wiping away your sadness sorrows despairs addictions sickness illness diseases hurts upsets burdens heartache pain suffering grievances always and forevermore. God is using you with your impossible battles you are struggling with and suffering with. To help bless reward restore replenish renew support build you up uplift exalt sustain give you and other people God's Special Knowledge hope courage inspiration insights truths laws revelations. God has allowed everything you suffer with. To help teach bless reward support guide other people. To God's Special Knowledge. Don't judge people with what they suffer with. Everyone suffers with some impossible battle in their life. God will save you from everything. God won't ever forsake you abandon you leave you. God loves you.

Your faith love hope in God. Is becoming increasingly more powerful through your trials and suffering. God is always and forever with you. God will give you positivity and hope when you feel hopeless. God will pick you up when you are down hearted. God always and forever loves you and adores you completely. God will fill up your spirit with God's power of the holy spirit. God will heal you from everything that is troubling you. God will place God's strength courage positivity hope into your spirit. When you feel hopeless in your circumstances. God will bless you and reward you with God's unconditional love kindness goodness forgiveness hope compassion sympathy empathy truths insights laws revelations God's Special Knowledge. God is love.

God is always for you. When people are against you. God will be there for you. When people reject you. God won't ever leave you alone. When people let you down hurt you disappoint you. God will bless help reward support prosper sustain fulfill love be with you. God will make you courageous bold daring sublime strong willed uplifted upbeat positive loving forgiving compassionate sympathetic empathetic powerful. Through the power of the holy spirit where God dwells within you spirit always and forevermore.God is there.

God is with you when people are against you. God will fill that empty void you are missing within your spirit. With the powerful presence of God's holy spirit within your heart and soul. God loves to bless and reward God's Precious Children always and forever. Pray to God God will answer all of your prayers in God's Perfect and Amazing Timing. God will perform the most incredible amazing out of this world great sublime powerful miraculous supernatural miracles wonders surprises delights upon you. God will make you the happiest you have ever been in your life. The power of the holy spirit where God dwells within your heart and soul. Will deliver you from everything.

www.ingramcontent.com/pod-product-compliance
Lightning Source LLC
Chambersburg PA
CBHW030316130626
46549CB00002B/878